Two Plays

THE DILEMMA
OF A GHOST

ANOWA

Ama Ata Aidoo

LONGMAN

Addison Wesley Longman Limited
Edinburgh Gate, Harlow,
Essex CM20 2JE, England
and Associated Companies throughout the world.

Longman Publishing Group
10 Bank Street
White Plains
New York 10601-1951
USA

Canadian stockist
Copp Clark Pitman Ltd
2775 Matheson Blvd East
Mississauga
Ontario L4W 4P7
Canada

First published in Longman African Classic 1987
First published as Longman African Writers 1995
Fifth impression 1998

Set in 10/11 Baskerville (Linotron)

Produced by Addison Wesley Longman China Limited, Hong Kong.
PPLC/05

ISBN 0 582 27602 0

Contents

THE DILEMMA
OF A GHOST

To the memory of Papa

Characters

ATO YAWSON: [Ebow] *A young Ghanaian graduate*
EULALIE YAWSON (*née* RUSH): *Afro-American graduate*
ESI KOM: [Maami] *Ato's mother*
MONKA: *His sister*
NANA: *His grandmother*
AKYERE: *His elder aunt*
MANSA: *His younger aunt*
PETU: *His elder uncle*
AKROMA: *His younger uncle*
1ST WOMAN ⎫ *Neighbours*
2ND WOMAN ⎭
BOY ⎱ *Two children in a dream. The boy being the*
GIRL ⎰ *ghost of Ato's former self*

The Bird of the Wayside

The Dilemma of a Ghost was first presented by the Students' Theatre, Legon, on the 12th, 13th and 14th of March, 1964, at the Open-Air Theatre, Commonwealth Hall, University of Ghana, Legon.

The action takes place in the courtyard of the newest wing of the Odumna Clan house. It is enclosed on the right by a wall of the old building and both at the centre and on the left by the walls of the new wing. At the right-hand corner a door links the courtyard with a passage that leads into the much bigger courtyard of the old house. In the middle of the left wall there is a door leading into the new rooms. A terrace runs round the two sides of the new sector.

In the foreground is the path which links the roads leading to the river, the farm and the market.

Prelude

I am the Bird of the Wayside—
The sudden scampering in the undergrowth,
Or the trunkless head
Of the shadow in the corner.
I am an asthmatic old hag
Eternally breaking the nuts
Whose soup, alas,
Nourished a bundle of whitened bones—
Or a pair of women, your neighbours
Chattering their lives away.
I can furnish you with reasons why
This and that and other things
Happened. But stranger,
What would you have me say
About the Odumna Clan?…
Look around you,
For the mouth must not tell everything.
Sometimes the eye can see
And the ear should hear.
Yonder house is larger than
Any in the town—
Old as the names
Oburumankuma, Odapadjan, Osun.
They multiply faster than fowls
And they acquire gold
As if it were corn grains—
But if in the making of
One Scholar
Much is gone
You stranger do not know.
Just you listen to their horn-blower:
    'We came from left
    We came from right
    We came from left
    We came from right

> The twig shall not pierce our eyes
> Nor the rivers prevail o'er us.
> We are of the vanguard
> We are running forward, forward, forward...'

Thus, it is only to be expected that they should reserve the new addition to the house for the exclusive use of the One Scholar. Not that they expect him to make his home there. No ... he will certainly have to live and work in the city when he arrives from the white man's land.

But they all expect him to come down, now and then, at the weekend and on festive occasions like Christmas. And certainly, he must come home for blessings when the new yam has been harvested and the Stools are sprinkled. The ghosts of the dead ancestors are invoked and there is no discord, only harmony and a restoration of that which needs to be restored. But the Day of Planning is different from the Day of Battle. And when the One Scholar came ... I cannot tell you what happened. You shall see that anon. But it all began on a University Campus; never mind where. The evening was cool as evenings are. Darkness was approaching when I heard the voices of a man and woman speaking ...

EU: Graduation! Ah well, that too isn't bad. But who's a graduate? What sort of creature is it? Why should I have supposed that mere graduation is a passport to happiness?

ATO: [*Harshly*] If you must know, woman, I think you do get on my nerves. Since you do not think much of a degree, why for heaven's sake did you go in for it?

EU: Don't shout at me, if you please.

ATO: Do keep your mouth shut, if you please.

EU: I suppose African women don't talk?

ATO: How often do you want to drag in about African women? Leave them alone, will you ... Ah yes they talk. But Christ, they don't run on in this way. This running-tap drawl gets on my nerves.

EU: What do you mean?

ATO: I mean exactly what I said.

EU: Look here, I don't think that I'll stand by and have you say I am not as good as your folks.

ATO: But what have I said, for goodness sake?

EU: Well, what did you mean by running-tap drawl? I only speak like I was born to speak—like an American!

ATO: [*Contrite*] Nonsense, darling ... But Sweetie Pie, can't we ever talk, but we must drag in the differences between your people and mine? Darling, we'll be happy, won't we?

EU: [*Relaxing*] I'm optimistic, Native Boy. To belong to somewhere again ... Sure, this must be bliss.

ATO: Poor Sweetie Pie.

EU: But I will not be poor again, will I? I'll just be 'Sweetie Pie'. Waw! The palm trees, the azure sea, the sun and golden beaches ...

ATO: Steady, woman. Where did you get hold of a tourist brochure? There are no palms where we will live. There are coconut trees ... coconut palms, though. Unless of course if I take you to see my folks at home. There are real palm trees there.

EU: Ah well, I don't know the difference, and I don't care neither. Coconut palms, palm-palms, aren't they all the same? And anyway, why should I not go and see your folks?

ATO: You may not be impressed.

EU: Silly darling. Who wants to be impressed? Fine folks Eulalie Rush has herself, eh? Could I even point to you a beggar in the streets as my father or mother? Ato, can't your Ma be sort of my Ma too?

ATO: [*Slowly and uncertainly*] Sure she can.

EU: And your Pa mine?

ATO: Sure.

[*Following lines solemn, like a prayer*]

And all my people your people ...

EU: And your gods my gods?

ATO: Yes.

EU: Shall I die where you will die?

ATO: Yes … And if you want to, you shall be buried there also. [*Pause*]

EU: [*Anxiously*] But darling, I really hope it won't matter at all?

ATO: What?

EU: You know what, Native Boy.

ATO: 'Lalie, don't you believe me when I tell you it's O.K.? I love you, Eulalie, and that's what matters. Your own sweet self should be O.K. for any guy. And how can a first-born child be difficult to please? Children, who wants them? In fact, they will make me jealous. I couldn't bear seeing you love someone else better than you do me. Not yet, darling, and not even my own children.

EU: You really sure?

ATO: Aren't you the sweetest and loveliest things in Africa and America rolled together? My darling, we are going to create a paradise, with or without children.

EU: Darling, some men do mind a lot.

ATO: [*Vehemently*] Look at me, we shall postpone having children for as long you would want.

EU: But still, I understand in Africa …

ATO: … Eulalie Rush and Ato Yawson shall be free to love each other, eh? This is all that you understand or should understand about Africa.

EU: [*Delighted*] Silly, I wasn't going to say that.

ATO: Then forget about what you were going to say.

EU: [*Persistently*] I only hope it's O.K.

ATO: It shall be O.K.

EU: Ato!

Act One

Evening. The two village women are returning from the river with their water pots on their heads.

1ST W: Ah! And yet I thought I was alone in this …
    The lonely woman who must toil
    From morn till eve,
    Before a morsel hits her teeth
    Or a drop of water cools her throat.

2ND W: My sister, you are not alone.
    But who would have thought that I,
    Whose house is teeming with children,
    My own, my husband's, my sister's …
    But this is my curse.
    'Shall I do this when
    This and that have nothing to do?'
    No. And they all sit
    With their hands between their knees.
    If the courtyard must be swept,
    It is Aba's job.
    If the *ampesi* must be cooked,
    It is Aba's job.
    And since the common slave was away all day
    There was no drop in the pot
    To cool the parched throat.
    I am telling you, my sister,
    Sometimes we feel you are luckier
    Who are childless.

1ST W: But at the very last
    You are luckiest who have them.
    Take Esi Kom, I say.

[ESI KOM *enters from the door on the right with two stools which she puts on the centre of the stage. For the rest of the scene, she moves stealthily but swiftly in and out of the stage arranging six stools in preparation for the next scene.*]

11

2ND W: What has happened?

1ST W: You know her son
That was away beyond the seas
Is now come back?

2ND W: So, that explains the new paint. When?

1ST W: Yesternight.

2ND W: Is he here?

1ST W: I do not know.

2ND W: I heard her younger children
Crying for eggs.

1ST W: Which means that those of us
Who are in this neighbourhood
Are going to have our mouths watering
With aroma of the fryings and stewings.

2ND W: Of course, that is what she always does.
And meanwhile the debts pile up.

1ST W: Yes, but the arrival of the son
May mean the paying of all the debts at last.
Her soul is a good one.

2ND W: Hmm. For my part, I would be ashamed
To live in a Clan house for
As long as she has done.
But let us hurry, my sister
For my food is getting cold.

[*They go out. After a minute or so,* ESI KOM *goes out too, having finished arranging the stools.*]

.   .   .   .

[*Later. It is quite dark now. The old woman totters in supported by her stick. In her youth, she had been a short, dark* petite femme *with a will like iron. Now, though she is weak, her tongue is as sharp if not sharper for her eighty plus. She sits on one of the stools in the centre of the stage. She props her chin on her stick. Presently* ATO *enters from the door on the left. For a few seconds the old woman continues sitting motionless as she has not seen him, then suddenly she speaks.*]

NANA: I am glad you came and found me alive.

ATO: I am glad too.

NANA: And what is on your mind, my grandson.

ATO: There is nothing else on my mind, Nana.

NANA: Were you not thinking, nay hoping, you will come and find me dead?

ATO: Oh!

NANA: Do not be pained my grand-child. I just wanted to trouble you a little. But go and tell your mother that if she and the others do not come early, I will be angry. [ATO *leaves by the door on the right.*] Already, naughty slumber is stealing over my senses. [*A clanging noise from within.*] Yes, someone has tripped in the doorway, eh. One day the people in this house will commit murder. Do they not know that if the heavens withdraw their light, man must light his own way? But no. They will let us all lie in darkness. How will he find his way around this dark place should the ghost of one of our forebearers pay us a visit? But this is something one should not speak about. They say they buy *kresin* and pay for it with money . . . as, as if the penny will shine and light our way when it is tied in a cloth . . . But of course, they will say I talk too much . . . Are they not coming? They are now removing their pans, tchia! Are these women? I shit upon such women. When we were young a woman cleared her eating place after the last morsel had hardly touched her tongue. But now, they will allow their nose-making pans to lie around for people to trip over. But it is not their fault. If they had to use earthenware pots which broke more easily than eggs, they would have learnt their lessons long ago.

ATO: [*From within*] Maami, why do not you and my Uncles hurry? Nana is getting impatient. [*He re-enters.*]

NANA: Have your Uncles Petu and Akroma come?

ATO: Yes, Nana. [*Voices from within.*]

MANSA: [*From within*] Oh, the old woman again!

NANA: But what are they doing there?

[*Several voices.* PETU *and* AKROMA *come in. The two men sit down.*]

13

PETU: Old woman, we greet you.

NANA: I respond, my Royal Ones. And how are you?

PETU: We are all well, Old One.

[ATO *slips into his room, left*]

NANA: Akroma, how is your wife's stomach?

AKROMA: It is a bit better.

NANA: I notice you do not feel clear in your own inside. You people always say I talk too much. So I try not to put my tongue in your affairs. But I hope you would think of what I always say. Have we not had enough of the white man's medicines? Since they do not seem to do anything for your wife, why do you not take her to Kofikrom? The herbalist there is famous . . .

AKROMA: I have heard you, Old One. I would put it to her people and hear what they have got to say too.

NANA: [*With her eyes turned towards the entrance*] I say, what are you doing there? Why are you doing this thing to me?

FEMALE VOICES: Ah, here we are. [ESI KOM, AKYERE *and* MANSA *enter. The stage is well-lit now. The women sit around on the terrace.*]

NANA: Ah, your characters are not pleasing. What were you really doing by the hearth. I thought you knew that I must not sit here until the dew falls on me.

MANSA: Old One, it is all right. We won't do this again.

AKROMA: But where is our master, the white man himself?

ATO: [*From within*] I am coming, Uncle. [*He comes out.*]

PETU: But where are you sitting? . . .

ESI: [*Overlapping* PETU *and directing her voice to the old sector*] Monka, are you not bringing your brother a chair?

MONKA: [*From within*] *Hei* Ebow!

ALL: What is it?

MONKA: [*Coming back with a chair*] The way some people became scholars is fearful.

ATO: What is the matter?

MONKA: The master scholar was sitting on the chair studying, so he could not move off! [ATO *laughs.*] After all, what is he learning? Is it the knowledge of the leopard skin?

[*Sucks her teeth.*]

ESI: If it had been in any other home, he, Ebow, would have seen to it that we were all seated.

AKROMA: But I do now know what he has done for all of you to pick on him in this way.

ESI: Let us say what we cannot keep in us any longer, for the day Ebow becomes like you, he will kick us all around as if we were his footballs.

NANA: Esi Kom, leave that child alone, for no one knows what the man of fame and honour was like when he was a child.

AKROMA: But Old One, we can soon know the bird which will not do well, for his nest hangs by the wayside.

ATO: Let us give him, too, some time.

MONKA: I always say that one can always know the man who is civilised.

NANA: I think you should all know that Ato was always a humble one.

PETU: Of course, he is a first born. Our eldest hold that first borns are always humble. Our white master, we welcome you.

ATO: I thank you, Uncle.

PETU: Ah, we have been here at home but you . . .

AKYERE: I say . . .

PETU: What is it?

AKYERE: I say, Esi. For a long time I have not been seeing that sheep which you were rearing in Ato's name.

AKROMA: As for you women.

ESI: Ho, I have sold it.

MANSA and AKYERE: Sold it!

ESI: But yes.

AKYERE: What did you do with the money?

ESI: [*Indirectly addressing* ATO] I have not done anything with it. It had a good market and I thought I would find some more money and add to it to give to Ato's father to pay for the bride price for its owner.

AKYERE: That is very good.

PETU: But women, can you not wait for us to finish what we came here to say? The child has just come from a

15

journey. You have not welcomed him but already you want to marry for him.

ATO: [*As if just awake from sleep*] Ei, Uncle, are you talking of marriage?

ESI: It is nothing. I was only telling your aunt that I have sold your sheep to pay the bride price for you when you make up your mind to marry . . .

ATO: [*Casually*] But I am already married, Maami.

ALL: You are married? Married! Married!

ESI: [*Overlapping*] Who is your wife?

AKYERE: [*Overlapping*] When did you marry?

MANSA: Who is your wife?

MONKA: [*Overlapping*] What is her name?

ESI: Where does she come from?

[*Everyone repeats her words to create confusion.*]

PETU: You must all be quiet. One must take time to dissect an ant in order to discover its entrails.

MONKA: [*Laughing wickedly*] Ei, so I have a sister-in-law whom I do not know?

AKROMA: *Ei*, Monka, keep quite.

NANA: [*Who has been sleeping since she last spoke*] What is all this noise about? Have you asked the child news from his journey?

[*Silence while everyone stares at* ATO]

PETU: Ato, when did you marry?

ATO: That is what I was going to tell you. One week ago.

NANA: [*Spitting*] My grand-child, so you have married? Why did you never write to tell us.

ESI: Ato my son, who is your wife?

ATO: [*Quite embarrassed*] Eulalie.

ALL: Eh!

ATO: I said 'Eulalie'. [*By now all the women are standing.*]

MONKA: Hurere!

ESI: Petu! Akyere! What does he say?

THE W: Hurere!

MONKA: Oh, let us say, let us say that some of the names that are coming into the world are fearful.

ESI: Ato, you know that some of us did not hear the school bell when it rang. Therefore we will not be able to say this name. This Uhu-hu . . . I want her real name, my son.

ATO: But Maami, this is her only name.

MANSA: Our master, isn't your wife . . . eh . . . Fanti?

ATO: No, aunt.

AKYERE: [*Contemptuously*] If so, what is her tribe?

ATO: She has no tribe. She does not come from . . .

NANA: [*Looking up at him*] She has no tribe? The story you are telling us is too sweet, my grand-child. Since I was born, I have not heard of a human being born out of the womb of a woman who has no tribe. Are there trees which never have any roots?

PETU: Ato, where does your wife come from? [*A short silence. All look at* ATO.]

ATO: But no one is prepared to listen to me. My wife comes from . . . America.

ESI: [*Putting her hands on her head*] Oh Esi! You have an unkind soul. We always hear of other women's sons going to the white man's country. Why should my own go and marry a white woman?

MONKA: Amrika! My brother, you have arrived indeed.

AKYERE: But we thought that we too have found a treasure at last for our house. What have you done to us, my son? We do not know the ways of the white people. Will not people laugh at us?

ATO: [*Very nervously*] But who says I have married a white woman? Is everyone in America white? In that country there are white men and black men.

AKROMA: Nephew, you must tell us properly. We do not know.

ATO: But you will not listen to me. [*All quite. Eyes are focused on* ATO.] I say my wife is as black as we all are. [*Sighs of relaxation.*]

ESI: But how is it, my child, that she comes from Amrika and she has this strange name? [*The old woman spits significantly.*]

NANA: Is that what people call their children in the white
man's country?

ATO: [*Irritably*] It is not the white man's country.

ALL: O . . . O . . . Oh!

ATO: Please, I beg you all, listen. Eulalie's ancestors were of
our ancestors. But [*warming up*] as you all know, the white
people came and took some away in ships to be slaves . . .

NANA: [*Calmly*] And so, my grand-child, all you want to tell us
is that your wife is a slave? [*At this point even the men get up
with shock from their seats. All the women break into violent
weeping.* ESI KOM *is beside herself with grief. She walks round in
all attitudes of mourning.*]

ATO: [*Wildly*] But she is not a slave. It was her grandfathers
and her grandmothers who were slaves.

NANA: Ato, do not talk with the foolishness of your
generation.

[*The two village women come into the path.*]

1ST W: My sister, what can be the meaning of this?

2ND W: That is what I cannot see.

1ST W: Probably the old woman is dead

2ND W: She has not been very well lately.

1ST W: This is life.
Some are going
While others are coming.
That is the road to the life hereafter.

2ND W: Then let us start weeping, my sister.

[*They begin to weep and walk up stage, then they notice* NANA.]

1ST W: Ah, but look, she is sitting there.

NANA: [*Hobbles towards the women*] Yes, I am sitting here. So
you thought I was dead? No, I am not. Go home good
neighbours and save your tears for my funeral. It cannot
be long now . . . Go.

[*The women turn back.*]

No, do not go yet, I still need your tears. [*All eyes turned on*

the women.] My grand-child has gone and brought home
the offspring of slaves. [*Women's faces indicate horror.*] A
slave, I say.

[ESI KOM *enacts horror and great distress.*]

Hear what has befallen our house.

ATO: [*Moving to the front of the stage*] Heavens! Is there any
reason why you should make so much fuss? All because I
have married an African-American? If you only know
how sweet Eulaie is! [*He look at the women and whistles.*]
Now all this racket you are putting on will bring the whole
town here. [*He turns back abruptly, goes to his door, enters and
closes it on the scene. All eyes are turned to the closed door now.*]

NANA: My spirit Mother ought to have come for me earlier.
Now what shall I tell them who are gone? The daughter
of slaves who come from the white man's land.
Someone should advise me on how to tell my story.
My children, I am dreading my arrival there
Where they will ask me news of home.
Shall I tell them or shall I not?
Someone should lend me a tongue
Light enough with which to tell
My Royal Dead
That one of their stock
Has gone away and brought to their sacred precincts
The wayfarer!

[*Everyone except* NANA *starts leaving the stage.*]

They will ask me where I was
When such things were happening.
O mighty God!
Even when the Unmentionable
Came and carried off the children of the house
In shoals like fish,
Nana Kum kept his feet steadfast on the ground

And refused to let any of his nephews
Take a wife from a doubtful stock.

[*She turns to leave, and walks towards the door on the right.*]

If it is true that the last gets the best of everything
Then what is this
Which my soul has drawn out for me?

[*Lights go out.*]

Act Two

[*A fortnight later. Afternoon. The two village women are returning from the woods where they have gathered some faggots.*]

2ND W: *Ei*, Esi Kom.
    Some child bearing is profitable.
1ST W: What has happened now?
2ND W: Nothing. It is only that I remember
    Her and her affairs when we pass their house.
2ST W: Child bearing is always profitable
    For were not our fathers wise
    Who looked upon the motion of our lives
    And said,
    They ask for the people of the house
    And not the money in it?
    There is nothing that can compare with
    Being a parent, my sister.
2ND W: Not always, my sister
    If you perchance hear on a silent afternoon
    The sound of a pestle hitting a mortar,
    Go get out your mortar too
    For they are only pounding cassava.
1ST W: Perchance they are pounding yam.
2ND W: Have you forgotten the daughter of this same
    Esi Kom? Have you not heard it whispered?
    Have you not heard it sung
    From the end of the East road
    To the beginning of the West
    That Monka never marries well?
1ST W: But if Esi Kom bears a daughter
    And the daughter finds no good man
    Shall we say
    It is Esi Kom's fate in childbirth,
    Or shall we say it is her daughter's trouble?
    Is not Monka the sauciest girl
    Born here for many years?

       Has she not the hardest mouth in this town?

2ND W: That is as it may
       But Esi Kom suffers for it.

1ST W: My sister, even from bad marriages
       Are born good sons and daughters.

2ND W: Who shall look after them?

1ST W: Do you ask that of me
       When everybody knows
       A son is back from the land beyond the seas?
       Shall he not help to look after his nephews
       And nieces when it was somebody else who
       Looked after him in the days of his childhood?
       You talk, my sister,
       As if the days are gone
       When the left hand washed the right
       And the right hand washed the left.

2ND W: Perhaps they are not, my sister.
       But those days are over
       When it was expedient for two deer
       To walk together,
       Since anyone can see and remove
       The beam in his eye with a mirror.

1ST W: These are sad sayings, my sister.
       But where is his wife?

2ND W: I do not know, my sister.
       But I heard them say that his mother
       Had gone to knock the door of Yaw Mensa
       To ask for the hand of his daughter for him.

1ST W: Oh, he would have had a good woman.
       I saw that girl when she came home last Christmas.
       School has not spoilt her, I think.

2ND W: And that is the sad part of it, my sister.
       He has not taken this girl
       Whom we all know and like,
       But has gone for this
       Black-white woman.
       A stranger and a slave—
       But that is his and Esi Kom's affair.
       I hear in the distance the cry of a child

That cry is meant for my ear.
Let us hurry home, my sister.

[*She takes the lead.*]

1ST W: Oh, Eternal Mother Nature,
Queen Mother of childbirth,
How was it you went past my house
   Without a pause
   Without a rest?
Mighty God, when shall the cry of an infant
Come into my ear;
For the sun has journeyed far
In my sky.
[*Lights out.*]

*   *   *   *

[*Late afternoon of the next day. Everywhere is quiet.* ATO *is asleep in the inner room.* EULALIE *comes in with a packet of cigarettes, a lighter, an ash tray and a bottle of Coca-Cola. She sits on the terrace facing the audience. She begins sipping the Coca-Cola and soon the voice of her mind comes across the courtyard. Later her mother's voice is also heard. As the voices speak on, her body relaxes except for her mouth which breaks into a light smile or draws up tightly; and her eyes, which stare in front of her or dart left and right generally expressing the emotions that her thoughts arouse in her.*] [*On the other hand the passage could be spoken as a soliloquy with the mother's voice interrupting from back stage.*]

VOICE: So at last here am I in Africa . . . Joseph and Mary! I
hope I've done the right thing. What good fun I'm going
to have here! [*Smiles.*] Just reckon, I hear the cottons are
exactly the thing! You hold on until I go to the shops . . .
[*She starts as she hears a rumble of drums*] . . . And anyway,
supposing this is just an ugly mess I've let myself into,
what am I going to do? You got a heart, Eulalie Rush?
No. Now it's over to you Eulalie Yawson . . . Yawson.

That surely is a name. [*Smiles.*] Life can be funny at times, that's what Fiona used to say. Now, I must sort of confess that I am finding all this rather cute. Ato says there will be two boys in the house. Fiona, if you could only see me now. [*Mouth grim.*] Or is it rather if I could only see you now? Sometimes a girl would just like to have someone she loves and knows to tell things to laugh with. But there is no one for me here who would have understood like you would, Fiona. There is no one even back in the States . . . Christ, Fiona, Pa and Ma! There was no one left was there? [*Bends her head.*] And how can one make a family out of Harlem? Ma . . . with her hands chapped with washing to keep me in College . . . I say [*Smiles*], I never knew there is Coke in these parts. [*Holding the Coca-Cola bottle affectionately.*] Fiona would have been shocked to hear it. How we used to talk of the jungle and the wild life . . . And I haven't seen a lion yet! As for his folks, they are cute. I adore the old one . . . His mother gives me a feeling, though. [*She starts and stares as she hears the drums again.*] Ma, I've come to the very source. I've come to Africa and I hope that where'er you are, you sort of know and approve. ' "Lalie", you shall not stop. Chicken, you must have it all.' And I had it all, Ma, even graduation. 'You'll be swank enough to look a white trash in the eye and tell him to go to hell.' Ma, ain't I telling the whole of the States to go swing! Congress, Jew and white trash, from Manhattan to Harlem . . . 'Sugar, don't let them do you in'. Ma, I didn't. 'Sugar, don't sort of curse me and your Pa every morning you look your face in the mirror and see yourself black. Kill the sort of dreams silly girls dream that they are going to wake up one morning and find their skins milk white and their hairs soft blonde like them Hollywood tarts. Sugar, the dear God made you just that black and you canna do nothing about it.' Ma, it was hard not to dream but I tried . . . only I wish you were not dead . . . I wish you were right here, not even in the States, but here in this country where there will be no washing for you no more and where . . . where . . . Oh Ma! But I know you would pat me on the back and say, 'Sugar, you sure done fine.' Native Boy is the blackest you ever saw . . .

[*Suddenly the drums just roll and roll.* EULALIE *throws away her cigarette, her eyes pop out. She is really scared. She mutters 'Christ, Christ', like a caged animal. She rushed towards the room and crashes into Ato's arms.*]

ATO: Hullo, my sweet. [*Then he notices her frightened look.*] What is the matter?

EU: Can't you hear?

ATO: Ah, what is it?

EU: Can't you hear the drums?

ATO: [*Cocks his ears*] Oh, those!

EU: Aren't you afraid? I am.

ATO: Don't be absurd, darling. [*Holds her close.*] But I thought that one thing which attracted you about Africa was that there is a lot of drumming here.

EU: [*Relaxes and thinks*] Y—e—s. But, you know, I didn't guess they'll be sort of like this.

ATO: You thought they would sound like jazz?

EU: Sure. Or rather like, you know, sort of Spanish mambo.

ATO: I see. [*Chuckles.*] But there is nothing specially frightening about this, is there?

EU: I don't know. I only thought it was witch-hunting.

ATO: What?

EU: Witch-hunting.

ATO: Witch . . . [*He bursts out laughing till he is quite breathless.*] Witch-hunting? O mine, who put that idea into your head?

EU: But I understand there is always witch-hunting out here in Africa.

ATO: But still, why were you so scared? You aren't a witch yourself, are you?

EU: Don't tease.

ATO: I'm not teasing. For after all, only a witch should be afraid of witch-hunting. For the rest of the community, it is a delightful sport.

EU: [*Curious*] How quaint? Tell me more.

ATO: I will, but first, you tell me: how were Hiawatha and
    Minehaha when last you met them?

EU: Now you are really teasing, Native Boy. But I thought I
    would learn about all these things.

ATO: [*Chuckles*] Especially witch-hunting? [*He takes her arm.*]
    Sorry, I don't know much about them myself. Those
    were only funeral drums. But I think you must have a
    siesta. If you don't, you'll have a nervous breakdown
    before you've learnt enough to graduate in primitive
    cultures . . .

EU: [*Looking up accusingly*] Native Boy.

[ATO *turns to look at her and sees the Coca-Cola bottle.*]

ATO: Have you been drinking Coke?

EU: Mm . . . Yes.

ATO: Excellent of you. I can't bear it warm.

EU: And of course you carried a refrigerator down here.

ATO: I am sorry.

EU: Christ, what are you apologising for? After all, I was only
    feeling a little homesick and I drank it for sentimental
    reasons. I could have had a much cooler, sweeter and
    more nourishing substitute in coconuts, couldn't I?

ATO: [*Confused and unable to say anything for some time*] I am
    thirsty too but I'll have a gin and water. [EULALIE's *eyes
    follow him as he goes back to the room and she is still looking in
    his direction when he returns some minutes later with the bottle of
    gin, water and a glass. He catches the look in her eyes and sits on
    the terrace facing her.*]

ATO: [*Mixing the drink*] Darling, what is it?

EU: What is what?

ATO: Well, there was such a look on your face. Were you
    going to say something?

EU: [*Gets up and moves closer to him*] Yes.

ATO: [*Lightly*] Box on then.

EU: Ato . . .

ATO: [*Interrupting*] By the way, are you interested? [*Indicating
    the gin and water.*]

EU: Yes.

ATO: Oh, I beg your pardon then. [*He gives her the mixture, and forgets about one for himself.*]

ATO: Aha—a.

EU: Ato, isn't it time we started a family?

ATO: [*Surprised*] Why? I thought . . .

EU: Ya, I remember I bought the idea, but I got the feeling . . .

ATO: Heavens, women! They are always getting feelings. First you got the feeling you needed a couple of years to settle down and now you are obviously getting a contradictory feeling.

EU: [*Her turn to look confused*] I hope you aren't taking it so . . . badly?

ATO: [*Boldly*] Not at all. It's only that I think we better stick to our original plans.

EU: [*Tiredly*] Okay! [*Long pause*] I'd better go and rest now.

[*She turns towards the door and the drink is entirely forgotten.* ATO *follows her into the room.*]

Act Three

[*Six months later. Saturday afternoon.* ATO *and* EULALIE *have come to spend a week-end. Her sunhat is lying on a chair in the courtyard. Two village children run in.*]

BOY: What shall we do now?
GIRL: *Kwaakwaa*
BOY: All right. I will hide, you find me.
GIRL: No, I will not find you, I will hide.
BOY: I say, I will hide.
GIRL: No, I will
BOY: I will not allow you
GIRL: Then I will not play
BOY: If you do not, I will beat you. [*Hits her.*]
GIRL: [*Crying*] Beast!
BOY: Oh, I did not mean to hurt you. But you too! I have told you I want to hide . . . Let us play another game then. What shall we do?
GIRL: Let us sing 'The Ghost'.
BOY: Ghost . . . Ghost . . . ah, yes! [*They hold hands and skip about in circles as they sing.*]
　'One early morning,
　When the moon was up
　Shining as the sun,
　I went to Elmina Junction
　And there and there,
　I saw a wretched ghost
　Going up and down
　Singing to himself
　　'Shall I go
　　To Cape Coast,
　　Or to Elmina
　　I don't know,
　　I can't tell.
　　I don't know,
　　I can't tell.'

[*They repeat, but halfway through the lights go out. When the lights come up a few seconds later, the children have vanished.* ATO *bursts in immediately. His hair is dishevelled, his trousers creased and his face is looking sleepy-eyed and haggard.*]

ATO: [*Looking right and left and searching with great agitation*]
Where are they? Where are those two urchins? Heavens! Those scruffy urchins and the racket of noise they were making. Why should they come here? But . . . Where are they? Or was it a dream? [*Panting*] Ugh! That's why I hate siesta. Afternoon sleep always brings me afternoon dreams, horrid, disgusting, enigmatic dreams. Damn this ghost at the junction. I loved to sing that song. Oh yes, I did. But it is all so long ago. I used to wonder what the ghost was doing there at the junction. And I used to wonder too what it did finally . . . Did it go to Elmina or to Cape Coast? And I used to wonder, oh, I used to wonder about so many things then. But why should I dream about all these things now?

[PETU *enters. He is in an old pair of trousers and a smock which make up his farm clothes.*]

Probably I am going mad?
PETU: Oh—o!
ATO: *Ei*, Uncle.
PETU: I heard you are come and that is why I am coming to greet you.
ATO: You went to the farm?
PETU: My master, where else have I to go? [*He sits on the terrace while* ATO *still stands.*] Since the morning has found us, we must eat. And as you know, some of us are not lucky enough to be paid only to sit in an office doing nothing. And that is why I have to relieve the wayside herbs of their dew every morning.
ATO: But my Uncle, we too work hard.
PETU: [*Sarcastic*] You believe that . . . But nephew, why were you talking so hard to yourself when I came in?
ATO: [*Uneasily*] I had had a queer dream.

PETU: Is that long ago?

ATO: No. It was only this afternoon when I lay down to rest.

PETU: An afternoon dream? [*His face shows he is not terribly pleased even about the idea of it.*] What was the dream?

ATO: I dreamt that there were two children in this courtyard singing that song about the ghost who did not know whether to go to Elmina or to Cape Coast.

PETU: Ah. [*He laughs.*] How funny!

ATO: But Uncle, the boy looked like me when I was a child.

PETU: [*Serious*] Ei, this needs thinking about. Do not be disturbed, although I do not like afternoon dreams myself. I will tell your grandmother and hear what she has to say about it. [*He rises to go and sees* EULALIE's *hat.*] Did you bring your wife?

ATO: Yes. She too is resting.

PETU: [*Turns towards the door on the right*] Yo—o. I am going now. When your wife wakes up, tell her I give her welcome. I have brought some cocoyams from the farm and I will be sending her some by and by. Do not think too much about the dream.

ATO: Thank you, my Uncle. When you go, tell my mothers that we will be coming to see them this evening. [PETU *goes away.* ATO *stands confused.* EULALIE *comes in.*]

ATO: Hullo, 'Lalie.

EU: Hullo. [*They kiss each other on the cheeks.*] I heard talking here, didn't I?

ATO: My Uncle came to give us welcome

EU: [*Anxious*] Oh, this means the whole lot of them will be coming to see us.

ATO: Would you rather we went to see the new Methodist School?

EU: Lovely [*She kisses him on the cheek again, and takes her lovely sunhat. She puts it on and cocks her head for admiration.* ATO *says 'Exquisite' and hand in hand they come down the courtyard following the path leading to the left.*]
[*Lights go off.*]

*   *   *   *

30

[*Two hours later.* ESI KOM *enters from the door on the right carrying two bundles wrapped in sack cloth. She opens the door to* ATO's *apartment. She puts the bundles in the outer room, comes out and is closing the door when* ATO *and* EULALIE *enter the courtyard from the path.*]

EU: [*Sees the woman*] I say! [*She glares at* ESI KOM *for a second or two and then turns on* ATO] Ato, would you care to ask your mother what she wants in our room?

ATO: Eh . . . Maami, were you looking for us?

ESI: Hmm . . . They told us when we arrived from the farm that you and your wife have come to spend today and tomorrow with us. So I thought I would bring you one or two things for I hear food is almost unbuyable in the city these days. And your nephews are so naughty that I knew if I did not bring them here they would steal the snails and roast them all in an hour's time.

EU: What is she saying?

ATO: Oh, she only brought us food to take back with us.

EU: What kind of food?

ATO: Maami, what did you bring?

ESI: Can not your wife herself go and see? After all, these are all women's affairs. Or do our masters, the Scholars, know what goes on in their wives' kitchen?

ATO: [*Persuasively*] Darling, will you go and check up, please?

[EULALIE *walks rather puzzled into the room. As she enters, she exclaims 'Sweet Jesus' and rushes out closing the door behind her.*]

ATO: Darling, what is it?

EU: Eh . . . some crawling things! [*Composing herself.*] Anyway, tell your mother we are very grateful.

ATO: Maami, my wife says she thanks you a lot for the things.

ESI: Tell her I am glad she likes them . . . Now, I think I will go and prepare the evening meal. Monka will cook you and your wife some rice and stew. If you need anything, you come and tell us or just shout for any of the children.

[*She turns off. Then turns back.*]

31

[*To* EULALIE] 'My lady', I am saying goodbye.

[*Accompanied by a wave of the hand.* EULALIE *waves back. The moment she is through the door on the right,* EULALIE *rushes to close it. Then she rushes into their room and brings out the sack bundle. She is crossing towards the path when* ATO *stops her.*]

ATO: What's all this?

EU: Those horrid creatures of course!

ATO: Where are you taking them?

EU: Throwing them away, of course.

ATO: What rubbish.

EU: What do you mean? What rubbish? If you think I am going to sleep with those creatures, then you are kidding yourself.

ATO: But how can you throw them away just like that? Haven't you seen snails before?

EU: My dear, did you see a single snail crawling on the streets of New York all the time you were in the States? And anyway, seeing snails and eating them are entirely different things!

[*She turns off as if to go on.* ATO *reaches her in two strides. He grabs a part of the sack.*]

ATO: But at least, I could give them to my mother to cook for me alone.

EU: And give them the opportunity to accuse me of unadaptability. No, thank you. [*She wrenches the bundle from* ATO *and as she turns off,* MONKA *opens the door on the right door. Her eyes take in the scene.* EULALIE *hurries down and dumps the sack near the path. At the same time,* MONKA *disappears closing the door on the right behind her.* EULALIE *and* ATO *just stare at each other.*]

MONKA: [*from within*] Maami, Maami, Ato's Morning Sunshine has thrown away the snails you gave them. [ATO *and* EULALIE *are still staring at each other when* ESI KOM *enters.*]

ESI: [*Addressing* ATO] Is it true that your wife has thrown away the snails I brought?

ATO: Who informed you?

ESI: That is not important, but is it true?

ATO: [*Defensively*] She does not know how to eat them . . . and . . .

ESI: And what, my son? Do you not know how to eat them now? What kind of man are you growing into? Are your wife's taboos yours? Rather your taboos should be hers.

[MONKA *re-enters and stands watching.* ATO *turns to her.*]

ATO: Yes, you went and told Maami, eh?

MONKA: Ei, take your troubles off me. Have you seen me here this afternoon?

ESI: These days, the rains are scarce and so are snails. But the one or two I get for you, you throw away.

[EULALIE *goes into their room.*]

ATO: But Eulalie . . .

MONKA: [*Derisively*] That's the golden name . . .

ESI: Yes, Hureri, Hureri . . . What does my lady say today . . .?

[EULALIE *comes back, sits on the terrace and starts puffing her cigarette.*]

MONKA: She reminds me of the words in the song:
    'She is strange,
    She is unusual.
    She would have done murder
    Had she been a man.
    But to prevent
    Such an outrage
    They made her a woman!'
Look at a female!

[EULALIE *ignores* MONKA *although her face shows she guesses at what is going on.*]

33

ESI: Hureri. Hmm. All the time I have been quiet as if I were a tortoise. But I have been watching, hoping that things would be different, at least, in this house.

ATO: [*Moving towards his mother*] Maami, this is only a small affair, what are you trying to say now?

ESI: What am I trying to say now?

MONKA: If nothing scratched at the palm fibre, it certainly would not have creaked.

ESI: If you listen, you will hear what I want to say. This is not the first time I have fallen into disgrace for bringing you things. Only it is my own fault. I should have learnt my lesson. The same thing happened the day I came to visit you at Accra . . .

ATO: Ah, are you still harbouring this grievance?

ESI: Do not annoy me, please. How can I forget it? I had travelled miles to come and visit you and your wife. And if you threw my gifts into my face and drove me out of your house, how can I forget it?

ATO: [*In desperation*] Maami, you make me too unhappy.

ESI: Listen to what he is saying.

ATO: We asked you and Monka to stay but you insisted on coming back.

MONKA: There are two kinds of offers. One which comes right from the bowels and the other which falls from the lips only. My brother, yours fell from your lips.

ESI: I had thought I would do as other women do—spend one or two days with my daughter-in-law, teach her how to cook your favourite meals. But as if I was not noticing it, neither you nor your wife bothered to give us seats to sit on or water to cool our parched throats . . .

ATO: I remember that Monka drank water.

MONKA: I begged for it!

ESI: . . . How can I then sleep in a house where I am not welcome? . . . Where did you throw the snails? [ATO *looks left and right uncertain of what to do.* MONKA *rushes to where* EULALIE *dumped the bundle and retrieves it.*]

MONKA: [*Coming back*] Here they are . . .

ESI: Bring them; at least we shall find a beggar to give them to. [EULALIE *makes as if to stand and speak but sits down again*

and continues puffing at her cigarette.]
Oh, Esi, of the luckless soul. It is true,
Living a life of failure is like taking snuff
At the Beach. Just consider the troubles I
Have had—the school fees, the uniforms . . .

MONKA: As for the balls of *kenkey*, they are uncountable.

ESI: The tears I have shed . . .

ATO: Must you go on in that way, Maami?

ESI: Keep quiet, my son and let me speak now, for something
has pricked my wound. My knees are callous with
bending before the rich . . . How my friends must be
laughing behind me now. 'After all the fuss, she is poorer
than ever before.'

MONKA: Even I should not be such a pitiable creature now,
after all, my brother is now a great man.

ESI: [*Overlapping*] Apart from the lonely journeys I made to
the unsympathetic rich, how often did I weep before
your Uncles and great Uncles while everyone
complained that my one son's education was ruining our
home.

MONKA: [*To herself*] I remember the time he was preparing to
go to the white man's land where he went to take up
[*indicating* EULALIE] this 'Wonder'! The money . . . the
money . . . This is something which no one should hear
anything about. A great part of the land was sold and
even that was sufficient for nothing . . . Finally, the oldest
and most valuable of the family heirlooms, *kentes* and
golden ornaments, which none of us younger generation
had ever seen before, were all pawned. They never
brought them into daylight . . . not even to celebrate the
puberty or marriage of a single girl in this house. But
since our master must buy coats and trousers, they
brought them out on this occasion. They were pawned, I
say. And have they been redeemed? When, and with
what? Ask that again.

ESI: For what do I still trouble myself, giving unacceptable
gifts? . . . I cannot get a penny to pay the smallest debt I
owe. Hureri must have eh . . . what do they call it?

ATO: Maami, is it not enough now? Give me time to work.

ESI: No, my son, I shall speak. You have been back a long time yet. The vulture, right from the beginning wallows in the soup he will eat. Have your Hureri got all her machines now? 'Hureri must have a *sutof*. Hureri must have something in which to put her water to cool. Hureri, Hureri. Oh, the name keeps buzzing in my head like the sting of a witch-bee! [*And with that she turns quickly off.* MONKA *turns to follow up, taking the sack with her.*]

MONKA: We are going. Ato, we wish you and your 'Morning Sun' a prosperous marriage. [*She too goes away, banging the door behind her. The couple are silent,* ATO *with a bowed head and* EULALIE *still puffing at a cigarette. Presently* ATO *speaks.*]

ATO: [*Quietly*] Now you have succeeded in making trouble for me. Won't you congratulate yourself? [EULALIE *continues to puff her cigarette. After what seems to be a long time, she puts the cigarette down, stamps on it, cries 'Blast' and gets up to go into the room.* ATO *comes out of the courtyard, and following the path on the left, walks ever so slowly into the night.*]

Act Four

[*Another six months later. The door to* ATO's *room is open. A great deal of noise comes over from the old sector of the house. The two women are on their way from the market where they have bought fish, pig's feet, seasoned beef, etc., for their evening* fufu.]

2ND W: My sister, do not say it loudly,
　　　Even fish is too dear to eat these days.
1ST W: If I think I have spent
　　　So much on fish . . .
2ND W: And what shall I say?
1ST W: Why is there so much noise from that house today?
2ND W: Do you not know
　　　Tomorrow is their 'Sprinkling of the Stools'?
　　　The son has come from the city.
1ST W: This reminds me of something
　　　I had wanted to ask these many days.
　　　If her son gets a goodly bag by the month
　　　Why has Esi Kom still not . . .
2ND W: I crave pardon
　　　For snatching the word from your mouth.
　　　But my sister, roll your tobacco and stuff your pipe.
　　　It has not been good going,
　　　The roof leaks more than ever before.
1ST W: But how can it be?
2ND W: If Nakedness promises you clothes,
　　　Ask his name.
1ST W: But I ask, how can it be?
2ND W: You ask me?
1ST W: But you know, my sister,
　　　That my name is Lonesome.
　　　I have no one to go and listen
　　　To come back and tell me.
2ND W: Then scoop your ears of all their wax
　　　And bring them here.
　　　Esi Kom is not better than she was.

1ST W: Why?

2ND W: They never ask 'Why'.
       Is it not the young man's wife?

1ST W: What has she done now?

2ND W: Listen, I hear she swallows money
       As a hen does corn.

1ST W: Oh, Esi Kom!

2ND W: One must sit down
       If one wants to talk of her affairs.
       They say that the young man gets
       No penny to buy himself a shirt . . .
       But the strangest thing is that
       She too works.

1ST W: Then how does she spend all that money?

2ND W: By buying cigarettes, drinks, clothes and machines.

1ST W: Machines?

2ND W: Yes, machines.
       Her water must be colder than hailstone.
       I heard it said in the market place
       Monka's teeth were set on edge
       For drinking water in her house.
       And her food never knows wood fire.

1ST W: Does she tear at it uncooked?

2ND W: As for you, my sister!
       She uses machines.
       This woman uses machines for doing everything.

1ST W: Is that why their money
       Never stays in their palms?

2ND W: But yes.

1ST W: This is very hard to understand.
       Before God-up-there
       My breasts have never given suck to a child,
       But if what I hear mothers say are true,
       Then the young people of the coming days
       Are strange . . . very strange.

2ND W: Fear them, my sister.
       If you meet them, jump to the wayside.
       Have I not born eleven from the womb here?
       I know what I am talking about.

1ST W: But this is too large for my head
  Or is the wife pregnant with a machine child?
2ND W: Pregnant, with a machine child?
  How can she be?
  Does she know what it is to be pregnant
  Even with a child of flesh and blood?
1ST W: Has she not given birth to a child since they married?
2ND W: No, my sister,
  It seems as if the stranger-woman is barren.
1ST W: Barren?
2ND W: As an orange which has been scooped of all fruit?
  But it is enough, my sister.
1ST W: Barren?
2ND W: One should not tell too much of a tale
  And we must eat tonight.
1ST W: Barren! . . .
2ND W: The mouth will twist that says too much of them.
  And as for her son's marriage,
  The ear will break that hears too much of it.
1ST W: Barren!
2ND W: I must leave you then.
  You know Esi Kom's troubles are many . . .
1ST W: Barren! . . .
2ND W: I say let us go. [*She takes the lead.*]
1ST W: Barren! . . .
  If it is real barrenness,
  Then, oh stranger-girl,
  Whom I do not know,
  I weep for you.
  For I know what it is
  To start a marriage with barrenness.
  You ought to have kept quiet
  And crouched by your mother's hearth
  Wherever that is—
  Yes. With your machines that cook
  And your machines that sweep.
  They want people.
  My people have a lusty desire
  To see the tender skin

On top of a child's scalp
Rise and fall with human life.
Your machines, my stranger-girl,
Cannot go on an errand
They have no hands to dress you when you are dead . . .
But you have one machine to buy now
That which will weep for you, stranger-girl
You need that most.
For my world
Which you have run to enter
Is most unkind to the barren.
And for you—
Who shall talk for the stranger?
My daughter or my sister,
Whom I have never set eyes upon,
You will cry until your throat is dry
And your eyes are blind with tears.
Yes, my young woman, I shall remember you.
I shall remember you in the hours of the night—
In my sleep,
In my sleepless sleep.

[*Lights go out.*]
[*Next morning.* PETU *enters with a wooden bowl full of white
and oiled* Oto (*mashed yam*), AKROMA *comes behind him
carrying a brass tray containing a herbal concoction and a kind
of sprinkling broom. They go round the courtyard sprinkling the
walls and the floor first with* Oto, *then with the potion. The
gong man beats the gong behind them. They circle thrice round
the courtyard and are just leaving when* PETU *calls to* ATO.]

PETU: Nephew!
ATO: [*Comes from the room and for the first time in cloth.*]
    Here I am, my Uncle.
PETU: We have killed the goats and chickens. The women will
    send you and your wife some of the *Oto* and then you can
    eat a proper breakfast. But do you not think you and
    your wife should come near the Stool Rooms?
ATO: *Yoo*, Uncle, We are coming.

PETU: But you are a man. So you must come and drink with
   the men first.

ATO: Then I am coming with you now.

[*He goes into the room and returns in a minute. They all leave
the courtyard by the door on the right.*]

[*Lights go out.*]

*   *   *   *

[*Several hours later,* EULALIE *enters from the door on the right.
She surveys the courtyard with disgust.*]

EU: What a blasted mess! Well [*She shrugs her shoulders.*] I
   suppose folks must have their customs. Though if you
   ask me, I think there has been enough messing round for
   one day. [*She goes into the room and returns with a glass of
   whisky and, as usual, a packet of cigarettes and a lighter. She
   lights her cigarette and moving to the door on the right, peeps out
   into the old apartment. She makes a face.* ATO *enters from that
   direction.*]

EU: [*Moving to him*] Native Boy, I have missed you dreadfully.

ATO: But you left us barely five minutes ago.

EU: That shows you that after a year of marriage I am still in
   love with my husband which, incidentally, is a wonderful
   achievement.

ATO: By what standards? Because I am still in love with my
   wife. [*They burst out laughing.* ATO *looks down at the glass in
   her hand.*] Sweetie Pie, don't drink too much.

EU: But I have not been drinking at all.

ATO: This looks too strong.

EU: I needed it so badly. I was getting rather nervy when I
   came back.

ATO: Well, now that I am back I don't think you need it, do
   you, Sweetie Pie?

EU: Just let me finish this. [*Voices behind the door to the right.*]

ATO: I think some of my people are coming. [*Anxiously*] Let
   me put your drink in the room for you.

EU: Why?

ATO: I don't think they'll approve.

EU: [*Taking a sip*] Nonsense. [*Voices draw nearer.*]

ATO: [*Trying to take the glass from her*] But 'Lalie, don't let them find you in the very act.

EU: [*Sarcastically*] Is this a taboo? [*She laughs and goes into the room. Just then,* PETU *and* AKROMA *enter followed by* MONKA *carrying the brass bowl containing the herbal concoction. Close behind her enter* ESI KOM, MANSA, AKYERE *and* NANA.]

ATO: Ei!

[*He gives the two chairs in front of the door to the two men who sit down. Everyone cries cheerfully to him* 'Afenhyiapa'. MONKA *puts her bowl down between the two men. The women sit round on the terrace.*]

ATO: [*Addressing* PETU] How is it I found you here, my elders.

NANA: [*From her corner*] Young man, one does not stand in ant-trail to pick off ants. You find somewhere to sit and then ask us for the purpose of the visit.

[ATO *hurries off into the room, returning with a chair on which he sits.*]

ATO: What brings you here this afternoon?

AKROMA: Aha, now you are moving in the right path, young man. If I am not putting my mouth into an affair which does not concern me, may I ask you where your wife is?

NANA: Who says it is not your affair? It's his affair, isn't it? [*Addressing this to* PETU.]

MANSA: If this isn't your affair, whose affair is it? It's everybody's affair isn't it? [*Addressing* AKYERE.]

ESI: *Ei*, these days, one's son's marriage affair cannot always be one's affair. [ATO *enters the room.*]

NANA: It may be so in many homes. Things have not changed here [*Knocking the ground with her stick.* ATO *returns with* EULALIE *who shows great surprise at seeing so many people around.*]

EU: But why so many people? [ATO *does not say anything.*

Everyone just stares at her. She looks round for somewhere to sit.
ATO *notices that and jumps to give her his chair.*]

PETU: And where shall you sit?

ATO: Oh, there. [*Indicating a place on the terrace. Cries of* 'Ei,
Odo *from the gathering.*]

PETU: Our master, we are going to talk to you and you must
be near enough to hear without our having to shout.
[ATO *looks with consternation at* EULALIE. *Their eyes meet and
they withdraw to aside where they have a tête-à- tête which is
inaudible to the audience. At the end,* EULALIE *walks away into
their room.*]

AKROMA: What has happened now?

ATO: Nothing Uncle.

PETU: Ah, is she going away?

ATO: Eh . . . eh . . . eh . . .

AKROMA: But what we are going to say concerns her.

ATO: Eh . . . since she will not understand it, you tell me and I
will tell her everything.

NANA: I have not heard the like of this before. Is the woman
for whom stalwart men have assembled herself leaving
the place of assembly?

ESI: Yet, this is something which must not be mentioned.

PETU: And if she leaves now, whose stomach shall we wash
with this medicine?

MONKA: Let us say! [*Followed by meaningful looks from the women
folk.*]

ATO: Uncle, did you say you are going to use the medicine to
wash my wife's stomach?

PETU: Yes.

ATO: Why?

AKROMA: Have patience, our master.

PETU: [*Looking round*] I hope I can deliver my message now.

ALL: Go on.

PETU: It was a couple of days ago that we met. What came out
of the meeting is that we must come and ask you and
your wife what is preventing you from giving your
grandmother a great-grandchild before she leaves us.
[*Everybody nods his/her head.* NANA *more violently than the
other.*]

ATO: Oh!

PETU: We were to choose this day because, as you know, on this day we try to drive away all evil spirits, ill luck and unkind feelings which might have invaded our house during the past year. You know also, that we invoke our sacred dead to bring us blessings. Therefore, we are asking you to tell us what is wrong with you and your wife so that first we will wash her stomach with this, then pour the libation to ask the dead to come and remove the spirit of the evil around you and pray them bring you a child.

ATO: [*Gripping his chair*] Good Heavens!

PETU: So my nephew, this is what we bring you. [*All eyes on ATO.*]

ATO: Oh!

AKROMA: Ato, they sent us to bring you a message and they asked us to take words from your own mouth to them. And I do not hope that you think we can go and tell them you only said 'Oh!'. What has been the cause?

ATO: Nothing . . . oh!

PETU: Haven't you got anything more to say? When two people marry, everyone expects them to have children. For men and women marry because they want children. Or I am lying, Akroma?

AKROMA: How can you be lying? It is very true.

PETU: Therefore, my nephew, if they do not have children then there is something wrong. You cannot tell us it is nothing. There is no disease in this world but it has a cure. It may cost a great deal, but money is worthless if it is not used to seek for people. If it is your wife . . .

ATO: [*Aggressively*] Why do you say it is my wife's fault?

PETU: Oh, my witness is your Uncle Akroma here. [*To AKROMA.*] Akroma, you heard me. Did I say it is his wife? All the words which came out of my mouth were 'If it is your wife . . .' How can I say it is your wife?

AKROMA: Petu could not have said that. Does he know what is in your marriage?

AKYERE: What sin would you have committed even if you said that?

ESI: I am very quiet.

AKYERE: Who does not know that she smokes cigarettes? And who has not heard that she can cut a drink as well as any man?

[*Cries of assent from all.*]

ATO: Heavens!
PETU: Nephew, we are still waiting.
AKROMA: He will say it is nothing.
PETU: What is wrong?
ATO: Nothing.
AKROMA: I told you so.
PETU: [*Angrily*] Monka, come carry the medicine. [*The women are too shocked. They stare vacantly.* MONKA *carries the brass bowl. They all stand up.*] Nephew, we will go our own way. I cannot be angry with you. I was only a messenger. Now, I remember your dream. I was going to ask the dead to come and take away the evil spirit which is haunting you. Now I know it is not a foreign evil spirit, my nephew. [*He strides out, followed by* AKROMA, MONKA *and the other women.* ESI KOM *turns back and, standing akimbo, stares at* ATO *for a long time. She only moves when the old woman turns back too and urges her to move, with her stick. But then she herself spits, before hobbling away.* EULALIE *peeps out and, discovering that the people are gone, comes out. She paces round for some time and then walks up to* ATO. *He does not stir.*]

EU: Native Boy, what did they say? [*Silence.*] Ato what's the matter?
ATO: They came to ask why we haven't started a family.
EU: And what did you tell them?
ATO: Nothing.
EU: What do you mean by 'nothing'? I should have thought the answer to that question is very simple.
ATO: They would say we are displeasing the spirits of our dead ancestors and the Almighty God for controlling birth . . .
EU: [*Bitterly*] You knew all this, didn't you, my gallant black knight? Now you dare not confess it before them, can you? [*She yawns*] Oh God! What an awful mess!

[*The lights go out.*]

Act Five

[*The next morning. Church bells are ringing in the distance. It is Sunday.* ATO *comes in wearing a mourning cloth. He is attending the Thanksgiving Service of a cousin, fourth removed, who had died the previous year. He walks up and down, obviously irritated.*]

ATO: [*Going to the door that leads to their room*] Eulalie, how long does it take you to put on a dress? [*There is no reply. He paces up and down*] I say Eulalie am I to wait here for ever?

[*Eulalie comes in wearing a house coat. She looks very excited.*]

EU: If you must know, darling Moses, I am not coming along.

ATO: What do you mean?

EU: You know what I mean, or don't you understand English neither?

ATO: [*Turning his back to her*] I am waiting for you. If we aren't there by nine, the place will be full up and I wouldn't care to stand through a whole Thanksgiving Service.

EU: Of course, you'd only have to come back here to sleep. [*She giggles.*] I would, only I repeat 'I ain't coming' eh. Or you are too British you canna hear me Yankee lingo?

ATO: [*Miserably*] Eulalie, you've been drinking!

EU: Sure, Moses.

ATO: Again? [*In a horrified voice*] And on a Sunday morning?

EU: Poor darling Moses. Sure, I have been drinking and on a Sunday morning: How dreadful? But surely Moses, it ain't matters on which God's day a girl gets soaked, eh?

ATO: [*Anguished*] Eulalie!

EU: Yeah . . . That jus whar yar beautiful wife as com teh, Soaking on God's holy day . . . My lord, whar a morning!

[*Hums 'My Lord what a Morning'.*]

ATO: [*Looking tenderly at her*] Sweetie Pie.

EU: [*Laughing again*] Ain't you going teh say Poor Sweetie Pie?

Ain't I poorer here as I would ave been in New York City? [*In pathetic imitation of* ATO] 'Eulalie, my people say it is not good for a woman to take alcohol. Eulalie, my people say they are not pleased to see you smoke . . . Eulalie, my people say . . . My people . . . My people . . .' Damned rotten coward of a Moses. [ATO *winces.*] I have been drinking in spite of what your people say. [*She sits on the terrace facing the audience.*]. Who married me, you or your goddam people?

[*She stands and moves closer to* ATO.]

Why don't you tell them you promised me we would start having kids when I wanted them?

ATO: They won't understand.

EU: Ha! And so you make them think I am incapable of having kids to save your own face?

ATO: It isn't that.

EU: Then what is it?

ATO: They simply won't understand that one should begin having children only when one is prepared for them.

EU: Sure not. What else would they understand but their own savage customs and standards?

ATO: Eulalie!

EU: And of course, you should have known that. Have they appreciation for anything but their own prehistoric existence? More savage than dinosaurs. With their snails and their potions! You afterwards told me, didn't you, that they wanted me to strip before them and have my belly washed? Washed in that filth! [*She laughs mirthlessly.*] What did you tell them I was before you picked me, a strip-tease? . . . [*She sits down again.*] Go and weep at the funeral of a guy you never knew. These are the things they know and think are worthwhile. [*At this point, she is certainly very sober.*]

ATO: Look here. I won't have you insult . . .

EU: . . . 'My people.' Add it, Moses. I shall say anything I like. I am right tired. I must always do things to please you and your folks . . . What about the sort of things I like? Aren't

47

they gotten any meaning on this rotten land?

ATO: [*With false forcefulness*] When in Rome, do as the Romans do.

EU: [*Contemptuosuly*] I thought you could do better than cliches. Since you can preach so well, can't you preach to your people to try and have just a little bit of understanding for the things they don't know anything about yet?

ATO: Shut up! How much does the American negro know?

EU: Do you compare these bastards, these stupid narrow-minded savages with us? Do you dare . . .? [*Like the action of lightning,* ATO *smacks her on the cheek and goes out of the house going by the path on the left.* EULALIE, *stunned, holds her cheeks in her hands for several seconds. She tries to speak but the words do not come. She crumples, her body shaking violently with silent tears, into the nearest chair. This goes on for a while and then the lights go out.*]

[*It is midnight of the same day.* ATO *stumbles from the path into the courtyard. He can barely see his way because it is very dark. As he comes along, he cries, 'Maami, Maami,' and goes to stand behind the door on the right. The two village women, each wrapped only in a bed cloth run into the path. They are carrying little tin lamps.*]

1ST W: My sister, what is it?

2ND W: Oh, are you awake too?

1ST W: Is this noise not enough to wake the dead?
Why so much noise at midnight?

2ND W: It is very dark.
I cannot make out the figure at the door,
It looks like a . . . ghost.
[*Tired,* ATO *crumples on the terrace.*]

1ST W: I think it is the son.

2ND W: Ah, you are right.

1ST W: But what does he want at this hour?

2ND W: I do not know, my sister.
But it seems as if
Between him and the wife

All is not well.

1ST W: How do you know?

2ND W: Oh, I could tell you
The bird of the Wayside
Never tires of chirping.
But this is no secret.
My sons tell me this:
On their way home
From laying their snares
They saw the lady wife
Sitting on the grass in the school
With her head bowed.

1ST W: Oh . . . And when was this, my sister?

2ND W: Just this evening.
Darkness was approaching.

1ST W: Unlucky prophecies coming true,
I could excel one
Who has swallowed the dog's eye.
… But what was she doing there?

2ND W: I do not know.
And it is not part of my worries.
Besides, marriage is like *Oware*
Someone is bound to lose
And another gain.

1ST W: But if both players are good,
The game may end equally.

2ND W: And how do you know
The players in this set are not equal?

1ST W: One has backers
Another has not!

2ND W: People have been known to win
Who even continue on other people's losses.

1ST W: You are right.
And this is only the beginning.

2ND W: If we know this
Then, my sister,
Let us go back to mend our broken
Sleep.

[*They leave.* ATO *gets up and starts pounding on the door again and at the same time keeps calling his mother.* ESI KOM *opens the door and comes out.* ATO *stares at her as she starts speaking.*]

ESI: *Hei,* what has happened that you wake folks from their beds? Is it very serious? Shall I go and call your uncles? Why did you and your wife not attend the Thanksgiving this morning? Where did you go? All the food we reserved for you is cold. Is it the custom of educated people not to bid goodbye when they are leaving people?

ATO: It is not that. Eulalie is gone.

ESI: [*Moving towards the front of the courtyard followed by* ATO] Where is she gone to?

ATO: I do not know.

ESI: [*Sighing*] Or is she gone to your house in the city?

ATO: I am coming from there.

ESI: Then where can she be? We thought the two of you went away together.

ATO: No.

ESI: But why should she behave in such a strange way?

ATO: I slapped her.

ESI: You slapped her? What did she do?

ATO: She said that my people have no understanding, that they are uncivilised.

ESI: [*Exclaims coolly and nods her head*] Is that it? [*She paces round then turns to* ATO.] My child, and why should your wife say this about us?

ATO: I do not know.

ESI: But do you never know anything? I thought those who go to school know everything . . . so your wife says we have no understanding and we are uncivilised . . . We thank her, we thank you too . . . But it would have been well if you knew why she said this.

ATO: [*Miserably*] I only asked her to come to the Thanksgiving with me. But she refused and . . .

ESI: And will she not refuse? I would have refused too if I were her. I would have known that I can always refuse to do things. [*A pause*] Her womb has receded, has it not?

But did you make her know how important it is for her to . . .

ATO: But her womb has not receded!

ESI: [*Unbelieving*] What are you telling me?

ATO: If we wanted children, she would have given birth to some.

ESI: *Ei,* everyone should come and listen to this. [*She walks round in all attitudes indicating surprise.*] I have not heard anything like this before . . . Human beings deciding when they must have children? [*To* ATO] Meanwhile, where is God? [ATO *is confused since he does not know how to reply to this*] . . . yet only a woman who is barren will tell her neighbours such a tale.

ATO: But it can be done.

ESI: *Yoo,* if it can be done, do it. But I am sure any woman who does it will die by the anger of the ghosts of her fathers—or at least, she will never get the children when she wants them.

ATO: But, Maami, in these days of civilisation . . .

ESI: In these days of civilisation what? Now I know you have been teaching your wife to insult us . . .

ATO: Oh, Maami!

ESI: Is this not the truth. Why did you not tell us that you and your wife are gods and you can create your own children when you want them? [ATO *is shamefaced and in spite of wide speculations and several attempts to speak, no words come out. There is a long pause.*] You do not even tell us about anything and we assemble our medicines together. While all the time your wife laughs at us because we do not understand such things . . . yes, and she laughs at us because we do not understand such things . . . [*Here, mother and son face each other for a long time and it is* ATO *who is forced to look down at last.*] . . . and we are angry because we think you are both not doing what is good for yourselves. [*She is almost addressing herself now.*] . . . and yet who can blame her? No stranger ever breaks the law . . . [*Another long puase.*] Hmm . . . my son. You have not dealt with us well. And you have not dealt with your wife well

in this. [ATO *make more futile attempts to speak.*] Tomorrow,
I will tell your grandmother, and your uncles and your
aunts about all this, and I know they will tell you that . . .
[*At this point* EULALIE *enters from the path on the right. She is
weak and looks very unhappy. She nearly crumples in front of
the courtyard while* ATO *stares dazedly at her. It is* ESI KOM *who,
following* ATO'S *gaze and seeing her, rushes forward to support
her on. After a few paces into the courtyard,* EULALIE *turns as if
to speak to* ATO. *But* ESI KOM *makes a sign to her not to say
anything while she herself continues to address* ATO . . .*] . . .
Yes, and I know
They will tell you that
Before the stranger should dip his finger
Into the thick palm nut soup,
It is a townsman
Must have told him to.
And we must be careful with your wife
    You tell us her mother is dead.
If she had any tenderness,
Her ghost must be keeping watch over
All which happen to her . . .
[*There is a short silence, then clearly to* EULALIE.]
Come, my child.

[*And with that,* ESI KOM *supports* EULALIE *through the door that
leads into the old house.* ATO *merely stares after them. When they
finally disappear, he crosses to his own door, pauses for a second,
then runs back towards the door leading to the family house,
stands there for some time and finally moves to the middle of the
courtyard. He looks bewildered and lost. Then suddenly, like an
echo from his own mind the voices of the children break out.*]

    Shall I go to Cape Coast
    Shall I go to Elmina?
    I can't tell
    Shall I?
    I can't tell
    I can't tell

I can't tell
I can't tell . . .

[*The voices fade gradually and the lights dim on him, gradually, too.*]

ANOWA

For my mother
'Aunt Abasema'
who told a story and sang a song

Cast

OLD MAN } *Being The-Mouth-That-Eats-*
OLD WOMAN } *Salt-And-Pepper*

A MAN AND A WOMAN: *who don't say a word*
ANOWA: *a young woman who grows up*
KOFI AKO: *her man who expands*
OSAM: *her father who smokes his pipe*
BADUA: *her mother who complains at the beginning and cries at the end*
BOY: *a young slave, about twenty years old*
GIRL: *a young slave girl*
PANYIN-NA-KAKRA: *a pair of boy twins whose duty it is to fan an empty chair*
HORNBLOWER
OTHER MEN AND WOMEN: *slaves, carriers, hailing women, drummers, messengers, townspeople*

Production Notes

Stage
Unless the producer has much ingenuity and can rely on speed, it is necessary for the stage to have parts to it, either at adjacent angles (right stage, left stage) or perpendicularly (upper stage, lower stage). The latter is what is maintained throughout the script and the doors are therefore upper left, upper right, lower left, lower right. The second stage could be narrower (smaller) than the first and, in fact, any space between the audience and the real stage can serve for this purpose.

Cast
The list is quite long but the scenes are such that one person can play two or more parts if necessary.

Costume
Anything African will do as long as a certain consistency is followed. Otherwise, a set of Ghanaian costumes might be made up of the following:
ANOWA: At the opening of Phase One she has a single piece of material about 2 yards long and 45 inches wide wrapped round her body. Later in Phase One she adds a similar piece to the original, having one tied round the lower half of her body and the other wrapped over her chest. In later scenes she may change the style of the second cloth and wear it like a shawl, or drape it round her shoulders and arms to express what she is feeling—cold, lonely or sad: but it should be the same pair of cloths throughout the play.
BADUA AND OLD WOMAN: Same as ANOWA in Phase One.
THE ANONYMOUS WOMAN OF PHASE ONE: An old cloth wrapped round her for a skirt, and an old-looking, old-fashioned cotton blouse, probably with pleated and fussy sleeves.
KOFI: In Phase One and first part of Phase Two he wears men's workclothes. These consist of a pair of long knickers and a jumper-shirt, both of them old-looking and possibly

patched. From the middle of Phase Two he is always in men's leisure clothes, for example a large piece of printed cotton (4 to 6 yards wide) worn around the whole body and the top edges gathered on the left shoulder. In the last part of Phase Two and throughout Phase Three, the Ghanaian *kente* (or any rich-looking fabric like velvet or silk) should be substituted; in these scenes, he should wear open sandals, a gold head band, rings and other gold jewelry (stage gold!).

ANONYMOUS MAN of Phase One, BOY and OTHER MALE SLAVES: Men's work-clothes.

OLD MAN AND OSAM: Men's leisure clothes.

Lighting

A skilled and extensive use of lighting could be very effective, especially to indicate the beginning and ending of scenes, since this helps to simplify the set and speeds up the movement of the play. Of course, the curtain of a conventional stage can always be used.

Libation

A realistic one may be poured only if it can be managed without clumsiness.

Music

As long as it would help to create the right atmosphere and comment on the action, the Ghanaian forms may be replaced by other African or any other folk music. The ATENTEBEN which is here intended as a symbol for ANOWA, is a single, delicate but wild wind instrument.

THE HORN (Bull's) is usually old and turned dark brown by sacrificial blood. It is an appendage of the stool and symbol of state, village or group power. An individual acquired a horn (but never a stool) if he felt he was rich and powerful enough. In fact, the acquisition of such a horn was a declaration of power. The horn sang the praises of its owner(s), its language codes being very similar to those of drums.

FONTONFROM: An essentially, dignified, low-rumbling drum in a big man's ensemble.

The Procession
It is not necessary to follow closely the instructions set down.
The important thing is to create an impression of opulence
and crowds; and the degree of the sumptuousness of the set
and for the whole of Phase Three should be managed to suit
the facilities available for any particular production.

Ending
It is quite possible to end the play with the final exit of
ANOWA. Or one could follow the script and permit
THE-MOUTH-THAT-EATS-SALT-AND-PEPPER to appear for the
last scene. The choice is open.

Prologue

[*Enter* THE-MOUTH-THAT-EATS-SALT-AND-PEPPER.

OLD MAN *always enters first from the left side of the auditorium.* OLD
WOMAN *from the right. Each leaves in the same direction. She is
wizened, leans on a stick and her voice is raspy with asthma and a
life-time of putting her mouth into other people's affairs. She begins
her speeches when she is half-way in and ends them half-way out. Her
entries are announced by the thumping of her stick, and whenever she
is the last of the two to leave the stage, her exit is marked by a
prolonged coughing. She is never still and very often speaks with
agitation, waving her stick and walking up and down the lower stage.
He is serene and everything about him is more orderly. He enters
quietly and leaves after his last statements have been made. The two
should never appear or move onto the upper stage. There is a block of
wood lying around on which the* OLD WOMAN *sometimes sits.*]

OLD MAN: Here in the state of Abura,
    Which must surely be one of the best pieces of land
    Odomankoma, our creator, has given to man,
    Everything happens in moderation:
    The sun comes out each day,
    But its heat seldom burns our crops;
    Rains are good when they fall
    And Asaase Efua the earth-goddess gives of herself
    To them that know the seasons;
    Streams abound, which like all gods
    Must have their angry moments and swell,
    But floods are hardly known to living memory.
    Behind us to the north, Aburabura
    Our beautiful lonely mountain sits with her neck to the
        skies,
    Reminding us that all of the earth is not flat.
    In the south, Nana Bosompo, the ocean roars on. Lord of
        Tuesdays,
    His day must be sacred. We know him well and even

65

The most unadventurous can reap his fish, just sitting on
   his pretty sands,
While for the brave who read the constellations,
His billows are easier to ride than the currents of a ditch.
And you, Mighty God, and your hosts our forefathers,
We do not say this in boastfulness . . .
[*He bends in the fingers of his right-hand as though he were
holding a cup, raises it up and acts out the motions of pouring a
libation.*] but only in true thankfulness,
Praying to you all that things may continue to be good
And even get better.
But bring your ears nearer, my friends, so I can whisper
   you a secret.
Our armies, well-organised though they be,
Are more skilled in quenching fires than in the art of
   war!
So please,
Let not posterity judge it too bitterly
That in a dangerous moment, the lords of our Houses
Sought the protection of those that-came-from-beyond-
   the-horizon
Against our more active kinsmen from the north;
We only wanted a little peace
For which our fathers had broken away
From the larger homestead and come to these parts,
Led by the embalmed bodies of the Three Elders.
And yet, there is a bigger crime
We have inherited from the clans incorporate
Of which, lest we forget when the time does come,
Those forts standing at the door
Of the great ocean shall remind our children
And the sea bear witness.
And now, listen o . . . o listen, listen,
If there be some among us that have found a common
   sauce-bowl
In which they play a game of dipping with the stranger,
Who shall complain?
Out of one womb can always come a disparate breed;
And men will always go

Where the rumbling hunger in their bowels shall be
    stilled,
And that is where they will stay.
O my beloveds, let it not surprise us then
That This-One and That-One
Depend for their well-being on the presence of
The pale stranger in our midst:
Kofi was, is, and shall always be
One of us.

[*First sign of* OLD WOMAN.]

But what shall we say of our child,
    The unfortunate Anowa? Let us just say that
    Anowa is not a girl to meet every day.

OLD WOMAN: That Anowa is something else! Like all the
beautiful maidens in the tales, she has refused to marry
any of the sturdy men who have asked for her hand in
marriage. No one knows what is wrong with her!

OLD MAN: A child of several incarnations,
    She listens to her own tales,
    Laughs at her own jokes and
    Follows her own advice.

OLD WOMAN: Some of us think she has just allowed her
unusual beauty to cloud her vision of the world.

OLD MAN: Beautiful as Korado Ahima,
    Someone's-Thin-Thread.
    A dainty little pot
    Well-baked,
    And polished smooth
    To set in a nobleman's corner.

[BADUA *enters from a door at upper right and moves down but
stops a few steps before the lower stage and stands looking at* OLD
MAN *and* OLD WOMAN.]

OLD WOMAN: Others think that her mother Badua has spoilt
her shamefully. But let us ask: Why should Anowa carry
herself so stiffly? Where is she taking her 'I won't, I

67

won't' to? Badua should tell her daughter that the sapling
breaks with bending that will not grow straight.

BADUA: [*Bursting out suddenly and pointing her fingers clearly at*
OLD MAN *and* OLD WOMAN *but speaking to herself*] Perhaps it
was my fault too, but how could she come to any good
when her name was always on the lips of every mouth
that ate pepper and salt?

[*She turns round angrily and exits where she had come from.*
OLD MAN *and* OLD WOMAN *do not show they had been aware of
her.*]

OLD MAN: But here is Anowa,
And also Kofi Ako.
It is now a little less than thirty years
When the lords of our Houses
Signed that piece of paper—
The Bond of 1844 they call it—
Binding us to the white men
Who came from beyond the horizon.

[*Exit* OLD MAN]

OLD WOMAN: And the gods will surely punish Abena Badua
for refusing to let a born priestess dance!

Phase One

IN YEBI

[*Lower Stage. Early evening village noises, for example, the pounding of fufu or millet, a goat bleats loudly, a woman calls her child, etc.* ANOWA *enters from lower right, carrying an empty water-pot. She walks to the centre of the lower stage, stops and looks behind her. Then she overturns the water-pot and sits on it facing the audience. She is wearing her cloth wrapped around her. The upper part of her breasts are visible, and also all of her legs. She is slim and slight of build. She turns her face momentarily towards lower left. During a moment when she is looking at her feet,* KOFI AKO *enters from the lower right. He is a tall, broad, young man, and very good-looking. The village noises die down.*

He is in work clothes and carrying a fish trap and a bundle of baits. He steals quietly up to her and cries, 'Hei!' She is startled but regains her composure immediately. They smile at each other. Just then, a WOMAN *comes in from the lower left, carrying a wooden tray which is filled with farm produce—cassava, yam, plantain, pepper, tomatoes, etc. Close behind her is a* MAN, *presumably her husband, also in work-clothes, with a gun on his shoulder and a machet under his arm. They pass by* ANOWA *and* KOFI *and walk on towards lower right. The woman turns round at every step to stare at the boy and girl who continue looking shyly at each other. Finally, the* WOMAN *misses a step or kicks against the block of wood. She falls, her tray crashing down.*

ANOWA *and* KOFI *burst into loud uncontrollable laughter. Assisted by her* MAN, *the* WOMAN *begins to collect her things together. Having got her load back on her head, she disappears, followed by her* MAN. *Meanwhile,* ANOWA *and* KOFI *continue laughing and go on doing so a little while after the lights have been removed from them.*

Upper Stage. The courtyard of Maami BADUA *and Papa* OSAM'S *cottage. Village noises as in previous scene. Standing in the centre is an earthen hearth with tripod cooking pot. There are a couple of small household stools standing around. By the right wall is a lie-in chair which belongs exclusively to Papa* OSAM. *Whenever he sits down, he sits in this. By the chair is a small table. The Lower Stage here* represents a section of a village side street from which there is an open entrance into the courtyard. In the background, upper left and upper right are doors connecting the courtyard to the inner rooms of the house.

In the pot something is cooking which throughout the scene Maami BADUA *will go and stir. By the hearth is a small vessel into which she puts the ladle after each stirring.*

BADUA *enters from upper right, goes to the hearth, picks up the ladle and stirs the soup. She is talking loudly to herself.*]

BADUA: Any mother would be concerned if her daughter refused to get married six years after her puberty. If I do not worry about this, what shall I worry about?

[OSAM *enters from upper left smoking his pipe.*]

Besides, a woman is not a stone but a human being; she grows.

OSAM: Woman, [BADUA *turns to look at him.*] that does not mean you should break my ears with your complaints. [*He looks very composed.*]

BADUA: What did you say, Osam?

OSAM: I say you complain too much.

[*He goes to occupy the lie-in chair, and exclaims, 'Ah!' with satisfaction.*]

BADUA: [*Seriously*] Are you trying to send me insane?

OSAM: Will that shut you up?

BADUA: Kofi Sam! [*Now she really is angry.*]

OSAM: Yes, my wife.

[BADUA *breathes audibly with exasperation. She begins pacing up and down the courtyard, with the ladle in her hand.*]

BADUA: [*Moving quickly up to* OSAM] So it is nothing at a—a—l—l [*stretching the utterance of the last word*] to you that your child is not married and goes round wild, making everyone talk about her?

OSAM: Which is your headache, that she is not yet married, or that she is wild?

BADUA: Hmm!

OSAM: You know that I am a man and getting daughters married is not one of my duties. Getting them born, aha! But not finding them husbands.

BADUA: Hmm! [*Paces up and down*]

OSAM: And may the ancestral spiritis help me, but what man would I order from the heavens to please the difficult eye of my daughter Anowa?

BADUA: Hmm! [*She goes and stirs the soup and this time remembers to put the ladle down. She stands musing by the hearth.*]

OSAM: As for her wildness, what do you want me to say again about that? I have always asked you to apprentice her to a priestess to quieten her down. But . . .

[*Roused again,* BADUA *moves quickly back to where he is and meanwhile, corks both her ears with two fingers and shakes her head to make sure he notices what she is doing.*]

OSAM: [*Chuckles*] Hmm, play children's games with me, my wife. One day you will click your fingers with regret that you did not listen to me.

BADUA: [*She removes her fingers from her ears.*] I have said it and I will say it again and again and again! I am not going to turn my only daughter into a dancer priestess.

OSAM: What is wrong with priestesses?

BADUA: I don't say there is anything wrong with them.

OSAM: Did you not consult them over and over again when you could not get a single child from your womb to live beyond one day?

BADUA: [*Reflectively*] O yes. I respect them, I honour them . . . I fear them. Yes, my husband, I fear them. But my only daughter shall not be a priestess.

OSAM: They have so much glory and dignity . . .

BADUA: But in the end, they are not people. They become too much like the gods they interpret. [*As she enumerates the attributes of priesthood, her voice grows hysterical and her face terror-stricken.* OSAM *removes his pipe, and stares at her, his mouth open with amazement.*]

71

They counsel with spirits;
They read into other men's souls;
They swallow dogs' eyes
Jump fires
Drink goats' blood
Sheep milk
Without flinching
Or vomiting
They do not feel
As you or I,
They have no shame.

[*She relaxes, and* OSAM *does too, the latter sighing audibly.* BADUA *continues, her face slightly turned away from both her husband and the audience.*]

BADUA: I want my child
To be a human woman
Marry a man,
Tend a farm
And be happy to see her
Peppers and her onions grow.
A woman like her
Should bear children
Many children,
So she can afford to have
One or two die.
Should she not take
Her place at meetings
Among the men and women of the clan?
And sit on my chair when
I am gone? And a captainship in the army,
Should not be beyond her
When the time is ripe!

[OSAM *nods his head and exclaims, Oh . . . oh!*]

BADUA: But a priestess lives too much in her own and other people's minds, my husband.

72

OSAM: [*Sighing again*] My wife, people with better vision than yours or mine have seen that Anowa is not like you or me. And a prophet with a locked mouth is neither a prophet nor a man. Besides, the yam that will burn, shall burn, boiled or roasted.

BADUA: [*She picks up the ladle but does not stir the pot. She throws her arms about.*] Since you want to see Nkomfo and Nsofo, seers and dancers . . .

ANOWA: [*From the distance*] Mother!

BADUA: That is her coming.

ANOWA: Father!

OSAM: O yes. Well let us keep quiet about her affairs then. You know what heart lies in her chest.

ANOWA: Mother, Father . . . Father, Mother . . . Mother . . . [OSAM *jumps up and confused, he and* BADUA *keep bumping into each other as each moves without knowing why or where he or she is moving.* BADUA *still has the ladle in her hands.*]

BADUA: Why do you keep hitting at me?

ANOWA: Mother!

OSAM: Sorry, I did not mean to. But you watch your step too.

ANOWA: Father!

OSAM: And where is she?

[ANOWA *runs in, lower right, with her empty water-pot.*]

BADUA: *Hei.* Why do you frighten me so? And where is the water?

ANOWA: O Mother. [*She stops running and stays on the lower stage.*]

OSAM: What is it?

ANOWA: [*Her eyes swerving from the face of one to the other*] O Father!

OSAM: Say whatever you have got to say and stop behaving like a child.

BADUA: Calling us from the street!

OSAM: What have you got to tell us that couldn't wait until you reached here?

ANOWA: O Father.

BADUA: And look at her. See here, it is time you realised you
   have grown up.

ANOWA: Mother . . . [*moving a step or two forward*]

BADUA: And now what is it? Besides, where is the water? I am
   sure this household will go to bed to count the beams
   tonight since there is no water to cook with.

ANOWA: Mother, Father, I have met the man I want to marry.

BADUA: What is she saying?

ANOWA: I say I have found the man I would like to marry.

OSAM: }
BADUA: }   Eh?

[*Long pause during which* BADUA *stares at* ANOWA *with her
head tilted to one side*]

ANOWA: Kofi Ako asked me to marry him and I said I will,
   too.

BADUA: Eh?

OSAM: Eh?

BADUA: Eh?

OSAM: Eh?

BADUA: Eh?

OSAM: }
BADUA: }   Eh—eh!

[*Light dies on all three and comes on again almost immediately.*
OSAM *is sitting in his chair.* ANOWA *hovers around and she has
a chewing-stick in her mouth with which she scrapes her teeth
when she is not speaking.* BADUA *is sitting by the hearth doing
nothing.*]

ANOWA: Mother, you have been at me for a long time to get
   married. And now that I have found someone I like very
   much . . .

BADUA: Anowa, shut up. Shut up! Push your tongue into your
   mouth and close it. Shut up because I never counted Kofi
   Ako among my sons-in-law. Anowa, why Kofi Ako? Of all
   the mothers that are here in Yebi, should I be the one
   whose daughter would want to marry this fool, this

74

good-for-nothing cassava-man, this watery male of all watery males? This-I-am-the-handsome-one-with-a-stick-between-my-teeth-in-the-market-place . . . This . . . this . . .

ANOWA: O Mother . . .

BADUA: [*Quietly*] I say Anowa, why did you not wait for a day when I was cooking *banku* and your father was drinking palm-wine in the market place with his friends? When you could have snatched the ladle from my hands and hit me with it and taken your father's wine from his hands and thrown it into his face? Anowa, why did you not wait for a day like that, since you want to behave like the girl in the folk tale?

ANOWA: But what are you talking about, Mother?

BADUA: And you, Kobina Sam, will you not say anything?

OSAM: Abena Badua, leave me out of this. You know that if I so much as whisper anything to do with Anowa, you and your brothers and your uncles will tell me to go and straighten out the lives of my nieces. This is your family drum; beat it, my wife.

BADUA: I did not ask you for riddles.

OSAM: Mm . . . just remember I was smoking my pipe.

BADUA: If you had been any other father, you would have known what to do and what not to do.

OSAM: Perhaps; but that does not mean I would have *done* anything. The way you used to talk, I thought if Anowa came to tell you she was going to get married to Kweku Ananse, or indeed the devil himself, you would spread rich cloth before her to walk on. And probably sacrifice an elephant.

BADUA: And do you not know what this Kofi Ako is like?

ANOWA: What is he like?

BADUA: My lady, I have not asked you a question. [ANOWA *retires into sullenness. She scrapes her teeth noisily.*]

OSAM: How would I know what he is like? Does he not come from Nsona House? And is not that one of the best Houses that are here in Yebi? Has he an ancestor who unclothed himself to nakedness, had the Unmentionable, killed himself or another man?

BADUA: And if all that there is to a young man is that his family has an unspoiled name, then what kind of a man is he? Are he and his wife going to feed on stones when he will not put a blow into a thicket or at least learn a trade?

OSAM: Anyway, I said long ago that I was removing my mouth from my daughter Anowa's marriage. Did I not say that? She would not allow herself to be married to any man who came to ask for her hand from us and of whom we approved. Did you not know then that when she chose a man, it might be one of whom we would disapprove?

BADUA: But why should she want to do a thing like that?

OSAM: My wife, do remember I am a man, the son of a woman who also has five sisters. It is a long time since I gave up trying to understand the human female. Besides, if you think well of it, I am not the one to decide finally whom Anowa can marry. Her uncle, your brother is there, is he not? You'd better consult him. Because I know your family: they will say I deliberately married Anowa to a fool to spite them.

ANOWA: Father, Kofi Ako is not a fool.

OSAM: My daughter, please forgive me, I am sure you know him very well. And it was only by way of speaking. Kwame! Kwame! I thought the boy was around somewhere. [*Moves towards lower stage and looks around*]

BADUA: What are you calling him here for?

OSAM: To go and call us her uncle and your brother.

BADUA: Could we not have waited until this evening or dawn tomorrow?

OSAM: For what shall we wait for the dawn?

BADUA: To settle the case.

OSAM: What case? Who says I want to settle cases? If there is any case to settle, that is between you and your people. It is not everything one chooses to forget, Badua. Certainly, I remember what happened in connection with Anowa's dancing. That is, if you don't. Did they not say in the end that it was I who had prevented her from going into apprenticeship with a priestess?

[*Light dies on them and comes on a little later.* ANOWA *is seen*

76

dressed in a two-piece cloth. She darts in and out of upper right, with very quick movements. She is packing her belongings into a little basket. Every now and then, she pauses, looks at her mother and sucks her teeth. BADUA *complains as before, but this time tearfully.* OSAM *is lying in his chair smoking.*]

BADUA: I am in disgrace so suck your teeth at me. [*Silence*] Other women certainly have happier tales to tell about motherhood. [*Silence*] I think I am just an unlucky woman.

ANOWA: Mother, I do not know what is wrong with you.

BADUA: And how would you know what is wrong with me? Look here Anowa, marriage is like a piece of cloth . . .

ANOWA: I like mine and it is none of your business.

BADUA: And like cloth, its beauty passes with wear and tear.

ANOWA: I do not care, Mother. Have I not told you that this is to be my marriage and not yours?

BADUA: My marriage! Why should it be my daughter who would want to marry that good-for-nothing cassava-man?

ANOWA: He is mine and I like him.

BADUA: If you like him, do like him. The men of his house do not make good husbands; ask older women who are married to Nsona man.

OSAM: You know what you are saying is not true. Indeed from the beginning of time Nsona men have been known to make the best of husbands. [BADUA *glares at him.*]

ANOWA: That does not even worry me and it should not worry you, Mother.

BADUA: It's up to you, my mistress who knows everything. But remember, my lady—when I am too old to move, I shall still be sitting by these walls waiting for you to come back with your rags and nakedness.

ANOWA: You do not have to wait because we shall not be coming back here to Yebi. Not for a long long time, Mother, not for a long long time.

BADUA: Of course, if I were you I wouldn't want to come back with my shame either.

ANOWA: You will be surprised to know that I am going to help

77

him do something with his life.

BADUA: A—a—h, I wish I could turn into a bird and come and stand on your roof-top watching you make something of that husband of yours. What was he able to make of the plantation of palm-trees his grandfather gave him? And the virgin land his uncles gave him, what did he do with that?

ANOWA: Please, Mother, remove your witch's mouth from our marriage.

[OSAM *jumps up and from now on hovers between the two, trying to make peace.*]

OSAM: *Hei* Anowa, what is wrong with you? Are you mad? How can you speak like that to your mother?

ANOWA: But Father, Mother does not treat me like her daughter.

BADUA: And so you call me a witch? The thing is, I wish I were a witch so that I could protect you from your folly.

ANOWA: I do not need your protection, Mother.

OSAM: The spirits of my fathers! Anowa, what daughter talks like this to her mother?

ANOWA: But Father, what mother talks to her daughter the way Mother talks to me? And now, Mother, I am going, so take your witchery to eat in the sea.

OSAM: *Ei* Anowa?

BADUA: Thank you my daughter. [BADUA *and* ANOWA *try to jump on each other.* BADUA *attempts to hit* ANOWA *but* OSAM *quickly intervenes.*]

OSAM: What has come over this household? Tell me what has come over this household? And you too Badua. What has come over you?

BADUA: You leave me alone, Osam. Why don't you speak to Anowa? She is your daughter, I am not.

OSAM: Well, she is not mature.

BADUA: That one makes me laugh. Who is not mature? Has she not been mature enough to divine me out and discover I am a witch? Did she not choose her husband single-handed? And isn't she leaving home to make a better success of her marriage?

OSAM: Anowa, have you made up your mind to leave?

ANOWA: But Father, Mother is driving me away.

BADUA: Who is driving you away?

ANOWA: You! Who does not know here in Yebi that from the day I came to tell you that Kofi and I were getting married you have been drumming into my ears what a disgrace this marriage is going to be for you? Didn't you say that your friends were laughing at you? And they were saying that very soon I shall be sharing your clothes because my husband will never buy me any? Father, I am leaving this place.

[*She picks up her basket, puts it on her head and moves down towards lower left.*]

BADUA: Yes, go.

ANOWA: I am on my way, Mother.

OSAM: And where is your husband?

ANOWA: I am going to look for him.

OSAM: Anowa, stop! [*But* ANOWA *behaves as if she has not heard him.*] Anowa, you must not leave in this manner.

BADUA: Let her go. And may she walk well.

ANOWA: Mother, I shall walk so well that I will not find my feet back here again.

[*She exits lower left.* OSAM *spits with disdain, then stares at* BADUA *for a long time. She slowly bows her head in the folds of her cloth and begins to weep quietly as the lights die on them. Enter* THE-MOUTH-THAT-EATS-SALT-AND-PEPPER.]

OLD WOMAN: *Hei, hei, hei!* And what do the children of today want? Eh, what would the children of today have us do? Parenthood was always a very expensive affair. But it seems that now there is no man or woman created in nature who is endowed with enough powers to be a mother or a father.

[OLD MAN *enters and walks up to the middle of the lower stage passing* OLD WOMAN *on the way.*]

Listen, listen. The days when children obeyed their elders have run out. If you tell a child to go forward, he will surely step backwards. And if you asked him to move back a pace, he would run ten leagues.

OLD MAN: But what makes your heart race itself in anger so? What disturbs you? Some of us feel that the best way to sharpen a knife is not to whet one side of it only. And neither can you solve a riddle by considering only one end of it. We know too well how difficult children of today are. But who begot them? Is a man a father for sleeping with a woman and making her pregnant? And does bearing the child after nine months make her a mother? Or is she the best potter who knows her clay and how it breathes?

OLD WOMAN: Are you saying that the good parent would not tell his child what should and should not be done?

OLD MAN: How can I say a thing like that?

OLD WOMAN: And must we lie down and have our children play jumping games on our bellies if this is what they want? [*She spits.*]

OLD MAN: Oh no. No one in his rightful mind would say that babies should be free to do what they please. But Abena Badua should have known that Anowa wanted to be something else which she herself had not been . . . They say from a very small age, she had the hot eyes and nimble feet of one born to dance for the gods.

OLD WOMAN: Hmm. Our ears are breaking with that one. Who heard the Creator tell Anowa what she was coming to do with her life here? And is that why, after all her 'I don't like this' and 'I don't like that', she has gone and married Kofi Ako?

OLD MAN: Tell me what is wrong in that?

OLD WOMAN: Certainly. Some of us thought she had ordered a completely new man from the heavens.

OLD MAN: Are people angry because she chose her own husband; or is there something wrong with the boy?

OLD WOMAN: As for that Kofi Ako, they say he combs his hair too often and stays too long at the Nteh games.

OLD MAN: Who judges a man of name by his humble beginnings?

OLD WOMAN: Don't ask me. They say Badua does not want him for a son-in-law.

OLD MAN: She should thank her god that Anowa has decided to settle down at all. But then, we all talk too much about those two. And yet this is not the first time since the world began that a man and a woman have decided to be together against the advice of grey-haired crows.

OLD WOMAN: What foolish words! Some people babble as though they borrowed their grey hairs and did not grow them on their own heads! Badua should have told her daughter that the infant which tries its milk teeth on every bone and stone, grows up with nothing to eat dried meat with. [*She exits noisily.*]

OLD MAN: I'm certainly a foolish old man. But I think there is no need to behave as though Kofi Ako and Anowa have brought an evil concoction here. Perhaps it is good for them that they have left Yebi to go and try to make their lives somewhere else.

[*As lights go out, a blending of the* atentenben *with any ordinary drum*]

Phase Two

ON THE HIGHWAY

[*The road is represented by the lower stage. A dark night. Wind, thunder and lightning.* KOFI AKO *enters from lower left. He is carrying a huge load of monkey skins and other hides. He looks exhausted and he is extremely wet from the rain.*]

KOFI AKO: [*Softly and without turning round*] Anowa [*Silence*]. Anowa, are you coming? [*There is no response from anywhere. Then, frenziedly,*] Anowa, *ei*, Anowa!

ANOWA: [*Also entering from lower left and carrying basket*] O, and what is wrong with you? Why are you so afraid? [KOFI AKO *turns round to look at her.*]

KOFI AKO: [*Breathing loudly with relief*] It is a fearful night.

ANOWA: But you do not have to fear so much for me. Why Kofi, see how your great chest heaves up and down even through the folds of your cloth! [*Laughs*]

KOFI: You just let it be then. [*She giggles more.*] And I can't see that there is anything to laugh at . . . Look at the lightning! Shall we sit here in this thicket?

ANOWA: Yes.

[*They move to upper stage, and stay in the central area.* KOFI AKO *puts his own load down with difficulty. He then helps* ANOWA *to unload hers and sits down immediately.*]

ANOWA: *Hei*, you should not have sat down in the mud just like that.

KOFI AKO: As if it matters. Now sit here and move nearer. [*He pulls* ANOWA, *shivering, down by him.*] Anowa, see how you shiver! And yet my tongue cannot match yours. [*Mocking her*] 'I am strong . . . O . . . O . . . It is not heavy. My body is small but I am strong!' *Ei*, Anowa!

ANOWA: But I am strong.

KOFI: We can see that. You know what? Shivering like this,

with all your clothes wet, you look like a chick in a
puddle.

ANOWA: And how about you? [*Beginning to rummage through
her basket as though looking for something*]

KOFI AKO: Do you compare yourself to me? See how big I am.
[*He bares his chest and spreads out his arms.*]

ANOWA: [*Pretending to be shocked*] Ahhh! And this is why we
should fear more of you. You are so tall and so broad.
You really look like a huge something. There is too much
of you. [*Touching different parts of him*] Anything can get
any part of you . . . a branch from a falling tree . . . a
broken splinter, and ow, my mouth is at the dung heap,
even lightning . . . But I am so little, I can escape things.

KOFI AKO: I was not born to die in any of these ways you
mention.

ANOWA: O seasoned Priest, and how was I born to die, that
you are so afraid of me?

KOFI AKO: I have no idea about that one. What I know is that
if you stay out longer in this weather, you are going to be
ill. And I cannot afford to lose you.

ANOWA: You will never lose me.

KOFI AKO: I thank your mouth.

[ANOWA *fishes out a miserable looking packet of food from the
basket.*]

ANOWA: Are you hungry? Here is what is left of the food. Oh,
but it is so wet. [*She giggles but gives it to him.*]

KOFI AKO: [*He clutches hungrily at the bundle.*] They are good.
How about you?

ANOWA: No, I am not hungry.

KOFI AKO: Perhaps you are ill already. [*Begins to wolf the stuff
down*] Mm . . . This life is not good for a woman. No, not
even a woman like you. It is too difficult. It is over two
hundred miles to the coast and I wonder how much we
have done. . . .

ANOWA: We are near Atandasu. this means we have only
about thirty miles or more to do . . .

KOFI AKO: Is that it? Do you know how many days we have been walking?

ANOWA: No, I have not been counting the days. All I know is that we have been on the highway for about two weeks now. [*Fights sleep*]

KOFI AKO: The ghost of my fathers!

ANOWA: But think of it, if we are not too tired to go a little further, we shall be there tomorrow.

KOFI AKO: Ei, Anowa. You ought to have been born a man.

ANOWA: Kofi.

KOFI AKO: Hmm . . . hmm?

ANOWA: Why don't you marry another woman? [KOFI AKO *registers alarm.*] At least she could help us. I could find a good one too [*Throws up her head to think*] Let me see. There is a girl in one of the villages we go to e . . . h . . . what is the name?

KOFI AKO: Anowa, please don't go on. You know you are annoying me.

ANOWA: Ah my master, but I don't understand you. You are the only man in this world who has just one wife and swears to keep only her! [*Silence*] Perhaps it is your medicine's taboo?

KOFI AKO: What medicine are you talking about? What taboo?

ANOWA: Ah Kofi, why has your voice gone fearfully down and so quickly?

KOFI AKO: But you are saying something about medicines and taboos which I don't understand. Were you not the same person who said we didn't need anything of that kind?

ANOWA: And if I said that, then it means from now on I must not mention medicines and taboos, not even in jest? Kofi [*Pause*] . . . what use do you think they will be to us? Who is interested in harming you or me? Two lonely people who are only trying something just because the bowels are not as wise as the mind; but like baby orphans, will shriek for food even while their mother's body is cold with death . . .

KOFI AKO: Anowa, the man who hates you does not care if you wait in the sun for your clothes to dry before you can go and join the dance.

ANOWA: But who hates us?

KOFI AKO: My wife, you speak as if we left Yebi with the town singing and dancing our praises. Was not everyone saying something unkind about us? Led by your mother? Anowa, we did not run away from home to go mushroom-hunting or fish-trapping.

ANOWA: I heard you, my husband. But I do not want us to be caught up in medicines or any of those things.

KOFI AKO: I too have heard you, my wife. Meanwhile, I am eating all the food . . .

ANOWA: Set your mouth free. Mine feels as though it could not stand the smell of anything.

KOFI AKO: [*Putting his hand on her forehead*] Anowa, please, don't be ill.

ANOWA: My mother has often told me that except for the normal gripes and fevers, my body has never known real illness.

KOFI AKO: Ah, but my wife seems to be extraordinary in more things than one. Anowa . . .

ANOWA: Yes?

KOFI AKO: We do need something to protect us. Even though no one dislikes us enough now to want to destroy us, how about when we begin to do well? Shall we not get hosts of enemies then?

ANOWA: [*Trying to keep voice light*] But my husband, why should we begin to take to our sick-beds now with illnesses that may affect us in our old age? Kofi, I just don't like the idea of using medicines.

KOFI AKO: But there are many things we do in life which we do not like—which we even hate . . . and we only need a bead or two.

ANOWA: But a shrine has to be worshipped however small its size. And a kind god angered is a thousand times more evil than a mean god unknown. To have a little something to eat and a rag on our back is not a matter to approach a god about.

KOFI AKO: Maybe you feel confident enough to trust yourself in dealing with all the problems of life. I think I am different, my wife.

[*For some time* ANOWA *quietly looks down while he eats.*]

ANOWA: Kofi, that was unkindly said. Because you know that I am already worried about not seeing signs of a baby yet.

KOFI AKO: It is quite clear that neither of us knows too much about these things. [*Pause*] Perhaps it is too early to worry about such a problem. We can consult a more grown-up person, but I know you would not like us to do anything like that.

ANOWA: [*Very loudly*] Listen to what he is saying! Is it the same thing to ask an older person about a woman's womb as it is to contract medicines in pots and potions which would attract good fortune and ward off evil?

KOFI AKO: I swear by everything that it is the same. And Anowa, it is too fearful a night to go screaming into the woods.

ANOWA: That is true.

[*More thunder and lightning.* ANOWA *begins to nod sleepily. Having finished eating,* KOFI *throws the food wrappers into the woods behind him. Then he notices* ANOWA *nodding.*]

KOFI AKO: Anowa, you are very tired. [*Jumping up*] Let me prepare somewhere for you to sleep.

[*Then he goes off-stage by upper right.* ANOWA *goes on nodding. Meanwhile the storm continues convulsively.*]

ANOWA: [*Startled awake by a peal of thunder*] What I am worried about are these things. [*She gropes towards the baskets and begins to feel the skins.*] See how wet they are. Tomorrow, they will be heavier than sheets of rock. And if it continues like this, they will all rot. Creator, [*she looks up*] do as you like, but please, let your sun shine tomorrow so we can dry out these skins. We must stop in the next village to dry them out. Yes, we must stop if the sun comes out.

KOFI AKO: [*Entering with a couple of plantain or banana leaves which he spreads out to form some kind of mat in the centre of lower stage*] To do what?

ANOWA: To dry out the skins. They are so wet

[KOFI AKO *concentrates on preparing the mat.* ANOWA *starts nodding again.*]

KOFI AKO: Eh? [*He turns round and sees her.*]

ANOWA: [*Mumbling*] The storm has ruined the whole corn field, Every stalk is down.

KOFI AKO: [*Moving with urgency, he picks her up in his arms*] Come Anowa, you are dreaming. Come to sleep. [*Carries her to the leafy bed*] Yes, Anowa, sleep well. Sleep well, and let every corn stalk go down. We shall not return to see the ruin [*Pacing up and down the length of lower stage*] Sometimes, I do not understand. Wherever we go, people take you for my sister at first. They say they have never heard of a woman who helped her husband so. 'Your wife is good' they say 'for your sisters are the only women you can force to toil like this for you'. They say that however good for licking the back of your hand is, it would never be like your palms. [*Pause*] Perhaps if they knew what I am beginning to know, they would not say so much. And proverbs do not always describe the truth of reality. [*His face acquires new determination.*] Anowa truly has a few strong ideas. But I know she will settle down. [*Addressing the sleeping woman*] Anowa, I shall be the new husband and you the new wife.

[*Now the storm is raging harder, thunder roars and lightning occurs more frequently. He stares at her for some time and then as lights begin to dim, he spreads out his big figure by her. Lights off. Pause.*]

When lights come on again, same scene without the leafy bed. The sun is shining and ANOWA *is spreading out skins from the baskets while* KOFI *stands looking on.*

Then ANOWA *holds her nose elaborately. Both of them burst out laughing. He moves in to help her.*]

KOFI AKO: Our noses are certainly suffering.

ANOWA: And yet what can we do? Without them, where would we stand?

KOFI AKO: Nowhere indeed.

ANOWA: [*Looking into one of the baskets and picking it up*] About two of them in here are too rotten to do anything with. [*She makes a movement of wiping sweat off her face, then yawns.*]

KOFI AKO: Come out of the sun. [*He takes the basket from her and places it away from them.*] Come, let's sit down in the shade. [*They go and sit near one end of the lower stage.*]

ANOWA: [*Breathing audibly*] Did your friend the doctor tell you what is wrong with me?

KOFI AKO: Yes.

ANOWA: What did he say?

KOFI AKO: I should have asked him whether I'm to let you know or not.

ANOWA: Ho! I think you can tell me, because he would not have forgotten to warn you, if he thought I should not know.

KOFI AKO: [*Quietly and with a frown*] He says there is nothing wrong with you.

ANOWA: Then why . . .?

KOFI AKO: Let me finish. He says there is nothing wrong with your womb. But your soul is too restless. You always seem to be looking for things; and that prevents your blood from settling.

ANOWA: Oh!

KOFI AKO: Anowa, are you unhappy. Do I make you unhappy?

ANOWA: [*With surprise*] No.

KOFI AKO: Perhaps this work is too much for you.

ANOWA: No. I think I have always been like that.

KOFI AKO: [*Alarmed*] Like what?

ANOWA: I don't know. I can't describe it.

KOFI AKO: Maybe you should stop coming on the roads.

ANOWA: [*Alarmed*] No. Why?

KOFI AKO: Why not?

ANOWA: I like this work. I like being on the roads.

KOFI AKO: My wife, sometimes you talk strangely. I don't see

what is so pleasing on these highways. The storms? The
wild animals or bad men that we often meet?

ANOWA: There are worse things in villages and towns.

KOFI AKO: Listen to her! Something tells me [*he stands up*] it
might be better if you stayed at home. Indeed I have
been thinking that may be I should eh . . . eh . . .

ANOWA: My husband, I am listening to you.

KOFI AKO: You remember, you were telling me to marry
another woman to help us?

ANOWA: Yes.

KOFI AKO: Hmm, I don't want to marry again. Not yet. But I
think . . . I think . . . that perhaps . . .

ANOWA: *Eheh!*

KOFI AKO: I think the time has come for us to think of looking
for one or two men to help us.

ANOWA: What men?

KOFI AKO: I hear they are not expensive . . . and if . . .

ANOWA: [*Getting up so slowly that every movement of her body
corresponds to syllables or words in her next speech*] MY
hus-band! Am I hear-ing you right? Have we risen so
high? [*Corking her ears*] Kofi Ako, do not let me hear these
words again.

KOFI AKO: [*Mimicking her*] 'Do not let me hear these words
again.' Anowa, do you think I am your son?

ANOWA: I do not care. We shall not buy men.

KOFI AKO: Anowa, look here. You are not always going to
have it your way. Who are you to tell me what I must do
or not do?

ANOWA: Kofi, I am not telling what you must do or not do . . .
We were two when we left Yebi. We have been together
all this time and at the end of these two years, we may not
be able to say yet that we are the richest people in the
world but we certainly are not starving.

KOFI AKO: And so?

ANOWA: Ah, is there any need then to go behaving as though
we are richer than we are?

KOFI AKO: What do you want to say? I am not buying these
men to come and carry me. They are coming to help us
in our work.

ANOWA: We do not need them.

KOFI AKO: If you don't, I do. Besides you are only talking like a woman.

ANOWA: And please, how does a woman talk? I had as much a mouth in the idea of beginning this trade as you had. And as much head!

KOFI AKO: And I am getting tired now. 'You shall not consult a priest . . . you shall marry again . . . we do not need medicines . . .' Anowa, listen. Now here is something I am going to do whether you like it or not. I do not even understand why you want to make so much noise about something like this. What is wrong with buying one or two people to help us? They are cheap . . . [*Pause.* ANOWA *walks around in great agitation.* KOFI AKO *continues in a strangely loud voice*] Everyone does it . . . does not everyone do it? And things would be easier for us. We shall not be alone . . . Now you have decided to say nothing, eh? Anowa, who told you that buying men is wrong? You know what? I like you and the way you are different. But Anowa, sometimes, you are too different. [ANOWA *walks away from him.*] I know I could not have started without you, but after all, we all know you are a woman and I am the man.

ANOWA: And tell me, when did I enter into a discussion with you about that? I shall not feel happy with slaves around . . . Kofi, no man made a slave of his friend and came to much himself. It is wrong. It is evil.

KOFI AKO: [*Showing alarm*] *Hei,* where did you get these ideas from? Who told you all this?

ANOWA: Are there never things which one can think out for oneself?

KOFI AKO: Yes, so now you are saying I am a fool?

ANOWA: [*Collapsing*] O the gods of my fathers!

KOFI AKO: What shall the gods of your fathers do for you? I know you think you are the wise one of the two of us.

ANOWA: Kofi, are you saying all this just so I will take a knife and go cut my throat?

KOFI AKO: Am I lying?

ANOWA: When and where and what did I do to give you this idea?

KOFI AKO: This is the way you have always behaved.

ANOWA: [*Her voice going falsetto*] Kofi! Kofi! [*He sits down by her.*] Hmm! Kofi, we shouldn't quarrel.

KOFI AKO: No, we should not.

[*The lights die on them and come up in a little while, on the upper stage. It is the courtyard of* BADUA's *and* OSAM's *cottage. It is early evening. Village noises.* OSAM *and* BADUA *are having their evening meal.* OSAM *is sitting in the lie-in chair, his food before him. He swallows a morsel.* BADUA's *food is on her lap. She is not eating. Presently she puts it down and gets up noisily. She turns right, she turns left. She begins to move around aimlessly, speaking at the same time.*]

BADUA: I haven't heard the like of this before. A human being, and a woman too, preferring to remain a stranger in other peoples' lands?

OSAM: [*Looking up from his meal*] Sit down, sit down. Sit down, and eat your food. [*Shamefaced,* BADUA *sits down.*] Hmmm, I was telling you. This child of yours . . . hm. . . . She was never even a child in the way a child must be a child.

BADUA: [*Turning round to face him*] And how must a child be a child?

OSAM: *Ei*, are you now asking me? I thought this is what you too have known all along. Ah, Nana, I beg you. Maybe that was not well said. [*Pause*] But I must say it has happened before us all. Has it not? Walked out of that door, she did, how long ago is that?

BADUA: Hmmm!

OSAM: … and has never been back since. I have always feared her.

BADUA: [*Shocked*] You have always feared hear? And is that a good thing to say about your own bowel-begotten child? If you fear her, then what do other people do? And if other people fear her then since a crab never fathers a bird, in their eyes, who are you yourself? After all, what has she done? She only went away with her husband and has not been back since.

OSAM: And that, you will agree with me, is very strange.

[*Guessing he might want a helping of the soup, she gets up and goes for his bowl.*]

BADUA: Yes, it is strange, but that does not make me say I fear her.

[*She takes the bowl to the hearth, and returns it to him after she has filled it.*]

OSAM: But don't other women leave their homes to go and marry? And do they stay away forever? Do they not return with their children to the old homestead to attend funerals, pay death debts, return for the feeding of their family stools? And Badua, listen here, if they did not do that, what would homes-and-homes do? Would not the clans break up for lack of people at home? The children of women like Anowa and their children-after-them never find their ways back. They get lost. For they often do not know the names of the founders of their houses . . . No, they do not know what to tell you if you asked them for just the names of their clans.

BADUA: Anowa has not yet had children.

OSAM: There you are. And is not that too strange? She has not had children. And barrenness is not such a common affliction in your family, is it?

BADUA: No, they have been saying it for a long time around here that she and her husband sold her birth-seeds to acquire their wealth.

OSAM: Of course, women have mouths to talk with. And indeed they open them anyhow and much of the time what comes out is nothing any real man can take seriously. Still, something tells me that this time she has given them cause.

BADUA: O Kofi Sam! [*She returns to her seat and places her bowl on her knee again.*]

OSAM: What have I done? I am not saying that they are right. But it certainly looks as if she and her husband are too

busy making money and have no time to find out and
cure what is wrong with her womb.

BADUA: Perhaps I should go and look for her.

OSAM: Go and look for her? How? Where? And anyway, who
told you she is lost?

BADUA: But she is my child.

OSAM: And so what? Do you think Anowa will forgive you
anymore for that? Please, leave her to live her life!

BADUA: Why are you always against me where Anowa is
concerned?

OSAM: You have been against me too. Did I not tell you to . . .

BADUA: —Make her a priestess . . . make her a priestess . . .
Always. Why? Why did everyone want me to put my only
child on the dancing ground? Since you want to see
possessed women so much, why didn't you ask your
sisters to apprentice their daughters to oracles?

OSAM: [*Very angry*] Don't shout at me, woman! Who comes
complaining to me about Anowa? . . . They say that that
would have been to the good of us all. But now—there
she is, as they said she might be, wandering . . . her soul
hovering on the outer fringes of life and always
searching for something . . . and I do not know what!

BADUA: [*Quietly*] I don't know what you mean by all this. Who
is not searching in life?

OSAM: I know you have just made up your mind never to
understand me.

BADUA: [*Bitterly*] Besides, that daughter of ours is doing well, I
hear. Yes, for someone whose soul is wandering, our
daughter is prospering. Have you heard from the
blowing winds how their trade with the white men is
growing? And how they are buying men and women?

OSAM: Yes, and also how unhappy she is about those slaves,
and how they quarrel from morning till night.

BADUA: So! I didn't know she was a fool too. She thought it is
enough just to be headstrong [*laughing drily*]. Before she
walked out that noon-day, she should have waited for me
to tell her how to marry a man. . . .

OSAM: Hmm.

BADUA: A good woman does not have a brain or mouth.

OSAM: Hmm. [*He coughs.*]

BADUA: And if there is something wrong with their slaves, why don't they sell them?

OSAM: That is not the problem. They say she just does not like the idea of buying men and women.

BADUA: What foolishness. People like her are not content to have life cheap, they always want it cheaper. Which woman in the land would not wish to be in her place?

OSAM: Anowa is not every woman.

BADUA: *Tchiaa!* And who does she think she is? A goddess? Let me eat my food. [*She goes to sit down and places the food back on her lap.*]

OSAM: And can I have some soup?

BADUA: Yes. [*As she gets up again, the lights die on the courtyard.*]

[*Eight men in a single file carrying skins enter by lower right, move silently up and across the main stage and away lower left. KOFI AKO follows closely behind them but stops in the centre of the lower stage. He is better dressed than before. He is carrying what seems to be a ridiculously light load. From off stage, ANOWA's voice is heard calling 'Kofi, Kofi'. He stops, she enters from the same direction, dressed as in the last scene although the lapse in time represents years. She is still barefooted. She is carrying nothing but a small stick which she plays with as she talks.*]

KOFI AKO: What is the matter?

ANOWA: Oh I just want you to wait for me.

KOFI AKO: Anowa, you walked faster when you carried loads which were heavier than mine.

ANOWA: Well, *you* took the load off my head. But don't you complain about my steps. I cannot keep up with you. These days you are always with your men.

KOFI AKO: [*Smiles*] Is that it? You know what? Let us sit down. [*They move to their position of the previous scene. Then as if he has remembered something, he moves some steps up towards the left and calls*] Boy!

BOY: [*Running in*] Father!

KOFI AKO: Tell the others that you are to sit down and rest a little.

BOY: Is our Mother coming to give us the food?

KOFI AKO: You can share it among yourselves, can you not?

BOY: We can, Father.

KOFI AKO: Then go and tell Yaako to share it up for you.

BOY: [*He leaves.*] Yes, Father.

KOFI AKO: [*Goes back to sit by* ANOWA] I think we should not come again with them. Yaako is very good and honest and he can manage everything.

ANOWA: [*Quietly*] Is that so?

KOFI AKO: I feel so.

ANOWA: [*Quietly*] Yes.

KOFI AKO: Why do you say that so sadly?

ANOWA: Did I say that sadly? Maybe I am sad. And how not? I cannot be happy if I am going to stop working.

KOFI AKO: But why, Anowa?

ANOWA: Men whom Odomankoma creates do not stop working . . . yes, they do but only when they are hit by illness or some misfortune. When their bodies have grown impotent with age.

KOFI AKO: Anowa, the farmer goes home from the farm . . .

ANOWA: [*Gets up and starts walking before* KOFI AKO] And the fisherman brings his boat and nets to the shore . . .

KOFI AKO: And if you know this already, then why?

ANOWA: They return in the morning.

KOFI AKO: But we have finished doing all that needs to be done by us.

ANOWA: Kofi, one stops wearing a hat only when the head has fallen off.

KOFI AKO: [*Irritably*] Anowa, can one not rest a tired neck?

ANOWA: Are we coming back after some time?

KOFI AKO: No

ANOWA: What shall we be doing?

KOFI AKO: Nothing. We shall be resting.

ANOWA: How can a human being rest all the time? I cannot.

KOFI AKO: I can.

ANOWA: I shall not know what to do with myself as each day breaks.

95

KOFI AKO: You will look after the house.

ANOWA: No. I am going to marry you to a woman who shall do that.

KOFI AKO: You will not marry me to any woman. I am not sending you on that errand.

ANOWA: See if I don't. One of these plump Oguaa mulatto women. With a skin as smooth as shea-butter and golden like fresh palm-oil on yam . . .

KOFI AKO: [*Jumping up and showing undue irritation*] Anowa, stop that!

ANOWA: Stop what?

KOFI AKO: What you are doing!

ANOWA: What am I doing? [*Pause*] Ei, master, let your heart lie cool in your chest.

KOFI AKO: Haven't I told you several times not to talk to me about marrying other women?

ANOWA: Hmm, I am quiet. [*Pause*]

KOFI AKO: [*Cooling down*] And if I marry again what will become of you?

ANOWA: Nothing that is unheard of. Ask your friends. What becomes of other women whose husbands have one, two, or more other wives besides themselves?

KOFI AKO: So what you want to be is my mother-wife?

ANOWA: Yes, or your friend or your sister. Have we not enough memories to talk about from our working days until we get tired of them and each other, when we shall sit and wait for our skins to fall off our bones?

KOFI AKO: Your mood is on. [*He stretches his left arm forward and looks at it intently.*]

ANOWA: [*Giggling*] What mood? You are always funny. My nothing is on. It is just that when I throw my eyes into the future, I do not see myself there.

KOFI AKO: This is because you have no children. Women who have children can always see themselves in the future.

ANOWA: Mm . . . children. It would be good to have them. But it seems I'm not woman enough. And this is another reason why you ought to marry another woman. So she can bear your children. [*Pause*] Mm, I am only a wayfarer, with no belongings either here or there.

KOFI AKO: What? What are you saying? Wayfarer, you? But are you talking about . . . about slaves . . . and you . . .? But, a wayfarer belongs to other people!

ANOWA: Oh no, not always. One can belong to oneself without belonging to a place. What is the difference between any of your men and me? Except that they are men and I'm a woman? None of us belongs.

KOFI AKO: You are a strange woman, Anowa. Too strange. You never even show much interest in what the oracles say. But you are not at fault; they all say the same thing. Anowa, what makes you so restless? What occupies you?

ANOWA: Nothing. Nothing at all.

KOFI AKO: [*Walking away from her*] Anowa, is it true that you should have been a priestess?

ANOWA: O yes? But how would I know. And where did you hear that from? [*Looking genuinely lost*]

KOFI AKO: Don't think about that one then. It doesn't matter. Still, there is too much restlessness in you which is frightening. I think maybe you are too lonely with only us men around. [*Pause*] I have decided to procure one or two women, not many. Just one or two, so that you will have companionship of your kind.

ANOWA: [*Almost hysterical*] No, no, no! I don't want them. I don't need them.

KOFI AKO: But why not?

ANOWA: No! I just do not need them. [*Long pause*] People can be very unkind. A wayfarer is a traveller. Therefore, to call someone a wayfarer is a painless way of saying he does not belong. That he has no home, no family, no village, no stool of his own; has no feast days, no holidays, no state, no territory.

KOFI AKO: [*Jumping up, furious*] Shut up, woman, shut up!

ANOWA: Why, what have I done wrong?

KOFI AKO: Do you ask me? Yes, what is wrong with you? If you want to go and get possessed by a god, I beg you, go. So that at least I shall know that a supernatural being speaks with your lips . . . [ANOWA*'s eyes widen with surprise*] I say Anowa, why must you always bring in this . . .

ANOWA: What?

KOFI AKO: About slaves and all such unpleasant affairs?

ANOWA: They are part of our lives now.

KOFI AKO: [*Shaking his head*] But is it necessary to eat your insides out because of them? [*Then with extreme intensity*] Why are you like this? What evil lies in having bonded men? Perhaps, yes [*getting expansive*] in other lands. Among other less kindly people. A meaner race of men. Men who by other men are worse treated than dogs. But here, have you looked around? Yes. The wayfarer here belongs where he is. Consorts freely with free-born nephews and nieces. Eats out of the same vessel, and drinks so as well. And those who have the brains are more listened to than are babbling nobility. They fight in armies. Where the valiant and well-proven can become a captain just as quickly as anyone. How many wayfarers do we know who have become patriarchs of houses where they used only to serve?

ANOWA: But in all this, they are of account only when there are no free-born people around. And if they fare well among us, it is not so among all peoples. And even here, who knows what strange happenings go on behind doors?

KOFI AKO: [*Irritated beyond words, he seizes and shakes her.*] Anowa, Anowa, where else have you been but here? Why can't you live by what you know, what you see? What do you gain by dreaming up miseries that do not touch you? Just so you can have nightmares?

ANOWA: [*Still cool, she stares at him*] It seems this is how they created me.

KOFI AKO: [*Letting go of her*] Hmm. How sad . . . And yet if I gave you two good blows on your cheeks which flashed lightning across your face, all this foolishness would go out of your head. [*To himself*] And what is wrong with me? Any man married to her would have by now beaten her to a pulp, a dough. But I can never lay hands on her . . . I cannot even think of marrying another woman. O it is difficult to think through anything. All these strange words! [ANOWA *continues to stare at him.*] Anowa, what is the difference? How is it you can't feel like

everybody else does? What is the meaning of this
strangeness? Who were you in the spirit world? [*Laughing
mirthlessly*] I used to like you very much. I wish I could rid
you of what ails you, so I could give you peace. And give
myself some. [ANOWA *still only stares at him.*] It is an illness,
Anowa. An illness that turns to bile all the good things of
here-under-the-sun. Shamelessly, you rake up the dirt of
life. You bare our wounds. You are too fond of looking
for the common pain and the general wrong.

[ANOWA *manages to look sad. She sighs audibly, then hangs
down her head as if ashamed. He looks down at her.*]

Anowa, you are among women my one and only
treasure. Beside you, all others look pale and shadowless.
I have neither the desire nor wish to marry any other,
though we all know I can afford dozens more. But
please, bring your mind home. Have joy in our
overflowing wealth. Enhance this beauty nature gave you
with the best craftsmanship in cloth and stone. Be happy
with that which countless women would give their lives to
enjoy for a day. Be happy in being my wife and maybe we
shall have our own children. Be my glorious wife,
Anowa, and the contented mother of my children.

[ANOWA*'s answer is a hard grating laugh that goes on and on
even after the lights have gone out on them.*
    The lights reappear after a little while. Enter THE-MOUTH-
THAT-EATS-SALT-AND-PEPPER. *First,* OLD MAN. *He walks up
to the centre of the lower stage, and for a short while, stands still
with his head down. Then he raises his head and speaks.*]

OLD MAN: My fellow townsmen. Have you heard what Kofi
    and Anowa are doing now? They say he is buying men
    and women as though they were only worth each a
    handful of the sands on the shore. *Ei*, Anowa and Kofi.
    Were those not the same who left Yebi like a pair of
    unwanted strangers? But peace creates forgetfulness and

money-making is like a god possessing a priest. He never
will leave you, until he has occupied you, wholly changed
the order of your being, and seared you through and up
and down. Then only would he eventually leave you, but
nothing of you except an exhausted wreck, lying prone
and wondering who you are. [*Enter* OLD WOMAN] Besides,
there must be something unwholesome about making
slaves of other men, something that is against the natural
state of man and the purity of his worship of the gods.
Those who have observed have remarked that every
house is ruined where they take in slaves.
As you sit,
They grow
And before you know
Where you are,
They are there,
And you are not.
One or two homes in Abura already show this;
They are spilling over
With gold and silver
And no one knows the uttermost hedges of their lands.
But where are the people
Who are going to sit on these things?
Yes,
It is frightening.
But all at once,
Girl-babies die
And the breasts of women in new motherhood
Run dry.

[OLD WOMAN *tries to get in a word, thumping her stick and
coughing.*]

OLD WOMAN: She is a witch,
   She is a devil,
   She is everything that is evil.
OLD MAN: [*Raising his head and showing interest*] Who?
OLD WOMAN: Who else but that child of Abena Badua?
OLD MAN: And what has she done now?

OLD WOMAN: Have you not heard? [*She is even more excited than ever. And for the rest of the scene makes an exhibition of herself, jumping, raising her stick in the air, coughing etc.*] She thinks the world has not seen the likes of her before. [*Now with feigned concern*] I wonder what a woman eats to produce a child like Anowa. I am sure that such children are not begotten by normal natural processes.

OLD MAN: [*With amused contempt*] But what?

OLD WOMAN: Ah! They issue from cancerous growths, tumours that grow from evil dreams. Yes, and from hard and bony material that the tender organs of ordinary human women are too weak to digest.

OLD MAN: Are you not sure that you are seeing too much in too little?

OLD WOMAN: What are you saying? Am I wrong? What woman is she who thinks she knows better than her husband in all things?

OLD MAN: A good husband would himself want advice from his wife, as the head of a family, a chief, a king, any nobleman has need of an adviser.

OLD WOMAN: But Anowa is too much. She is now against the very man who she selected from so many. She would rather he was poor than prospering. They say she raves hourly against our revered ancestors and sanctions their deeds in high tones. She thinks our forefathers should have waited for her to be born so she could have upbraided them for their misdeeds and shown them what actions of men are virtuous.

OLD MAN: I do not know if I can believe all this you say of the pitiful child. But certainly, it is not too much to think that the heavens might show something to children of a latter day which was hidden from them of old?

[OLD WOMAN *is so flabbergasted at this she opens her mouth wide and turns in the* OLD MAN's *direction while he walks slowly away.*]

OLD WOMAN: [*Closing her mouth in a heavy sigh*] But, people of Yebi, rejoice,

For Kofi Ako has prospered
And he is your son.
Women of Nsona house,
They say Kofi Ako can stand
On his two feet to dress up fifty brides
And without moving a step,
Dress up fifty more.
And where and when did this last happen
But in fables and the days of dim antiquity?
They say Kofi sits fat like a bullfrog in a swamp,
While *that* Anowa daily grows thin,
Her eyes popping out of her head like those of
A hungry toad in a parched grassland.
But she is the one
Who must not be allowed to step on any threshold here!
When was this infant born,
That would teach us all what to do?
Who is she to bring us new rules to live by?
It is good she said she was not coming back to Yebi,
But if she so much as crosses the stream
That lies at the mouth of the road,
We shall show her that
Little babies only cry for food
When hungry,
But do not instruct their elders how to tend a farm:
Besides,
As the sourest yam
Is better than the sweetest guava,
The dumbest man is
Always better than a woman.
Or *he* thinks he is!
And so Kofi shall teach Anowa
He is a man!

[OLD WOMAN *exits coughing and her throat wheezing.*]

Phase Three

THE BIG HOUSE AT OGUAA

[*The upper stage is a big central hall. The furniture here is either consciously foreign or else opulent. There are beautiful skins lying on the richly carpeted floor. Other articles include a giant sideboard on which are standing huge decanters, with or without spirits, and big decorative plates. In the central wall is a fireplace and above it, a picture of Queen Victoria unamused. To the left of the Queen is a picture of* KOFI AKO *himself, and to the right, a large painting of the crow, the totem bird of the Nsona clan. In the centre of the room is a gilded chair with rich-looking cushions, and in front of it, a leopard skin. the lower stage represents here a path leading from the house into the town and outside generally.*

The lights blaze on both lower and upper stages to a tumult which at first is distant but draws nearer and nearer to lower right. First a group of women, any number from four, enter from the right dancing to no distinct form and with great abandon. Meanwhile they sing, or rather recite.]

> He is coming!
> Nana is coming
> He is coming,
> The master of the earth is coming.
> Give way,
> O—o—give way!
> For the Master of all you see around is coming
> Turn your face, the jealous!
> Close your eyes, the envious!
> For he is coming,
> Nana is coming!

[*They pass on and away lower left, and after them, a lone man comes blowing* KOFI AKO'*s horn to the rhythm of just two lines*.]

> Turn your face, the jealous!
> Close your eyes, the envious!

[*The* HORNBLOWER *stops on the stage while multitudes enter
from the same direction and move away lower left. They are men
and women carrying raw materials, skins, copra, crude rubber
and kegs of palm oil. Controlling the exportation of the last
product has made* KOFI AKO *the richest man, probably, of the
whole Guinea Coast. Other men and women are carrying cheap
silks and madras cloth, muskets, hurricane lamps, knives and
enamel ware.*

    KOFI AKO *enters, borne by four brawny men in some kind of a
carrier chair, basket or sedan. He is resplendent in brilliant
kente or velvet cloth and he is over-flowing with gold jewelry,
from the crown on his head to the rings on his toes. He is
surrounded by more hailing women and an orchestra of horns
and drums. As he passes, he makes the gestures of lordship over
the area. The procession goes off, lower left; the* HORNBLOWER *is
the last man to leave.*

    When the tumult has died down, ANOWA *enters from upper
left and sits on one side of the chairs in the central hall. She looks
aged and forlorn in her old clothes. She is still bare-footed. She
sits quietly for a while, as though waiting for somebody, then she
stands up and begins to pace around, speaking to herself.*]

ANOWA: [*As she speaks, she makes childish gestures, especially with
her hands, to express all the ideas behind each sentence.*] I
remember once. I think I was very young then. Quite
young certainly. Perhaps I was eight, or ten. Perhaps I
was twelve. My grandmother told me of her travels. She
told of the great places she had been to and the
wonderful things she had seen. Of the sea that is bigger
than any river and boils without being hot. Of huge
houses rising to touch the skies, houses whose
foundations are wider than the biggest roads I had ever
seen. They contained more rooms than were in all the
homes I knew put together. Of these houses, I asked:
Tell me Nana, who built the houses?
She said:
Why do you want to know?
The pale men.
Who are the pale men?

I asked.
You ask too many questions.
They are the white men.
Who are the white men?
I asked.
A child like you should not ask questions.
They come from far away.
Far away from beyond the horizon.
Nana, what do they look like?
I asked.
Shut up child.
Not like you or me,
She said.
But what do they look like Nana?
I asked.
Shut up child or your mouth will twist up one day with
questions.
Not like you or me?
Yes like you or me,
But different.
What do they look like, Nana?
What devil has entered into you, child?
As if you or I
Were peeled of our skins,
Like a lobster that is boiled or roasted,
Like . . . like . . . but it is not good
That a child should ask questions.
Nana, why did they build the big houses?
I asked.
I must escape from you, child.
They say . . . they said they built the big houses to keep
the slaves.
What is a slave, Nana?
Shut up! It is not good that a child should ask big
questions.
A slave is one who bought and sold.
Where did the white men get the slaves?
I asked.
You frighten me, child.

You must be a witch, child.

They got them from the land.

Did the men of the land sell other men of the land, and
women and children to pale men from beyond the
horizon who looked like you or me peeled, like lobsters
boiled or roasted?

I do not know, child.

You are frightening me, child.

I was not there!

It is too long ago!

No one talks of these things anymore!

All good men and women try to forget;

They have forgotten!

What happened to those who were taken away?

Do people hear from them?

How are they?

Shut up child.

It is too late child.

Sleep well, child.

All good men and women try to forget;

They have forgotten!

[*Pause*]

That night, I woke up screaming hot; my body burning
and sweating from a horrible dream. I dreamt that I was
a big, big woman. And from my insides were huge holes
out of which poured men, women and children. And the
sea was boiling hot and steaming. And as it boiled, it
threw out many, many giant lobsters, boiled lobsters,
each of whom as it fell turned into a man or woman, but
keeping its lobster head and claws. And they rushed to
where I sat and seized the men and women as they
poured out of me, and they tore them apart, and dashed
them to the ground and stamped upon them. And from
their huge courtyards, the women ground my men and
women and children on mountains of stone. But there
was never a cry or a murmur; only a bursting, as of a ripe
tomato or a swollen pod. And everything went on and on
and on. [*Pause*]

I was very ill and did not recover for weeks. When I told my dream, the women of the house were very frightened. They cried and cried and told me not to mention the dream again. For some time, there was talk of apprenticing me to a priestess. I don't know what came of it. But since then, any time there is mention of a slave, I see a woman who is me and a bursting of a ripe tomato or a swollen pod.

[*She now stares straight and sharply at the audience for a long time, and then slowly leaves the stage by upper right. Then suddenly, the voices of an unseen wearied multitude begin to sing 'Swing Low, Sweet Chariot'. The song goes on for a while and stops. Long pause while lights remain on. Then the lights go off on the lower stage only.* GIRL *enters from upper right. She resembles* ANOWA *of a long time ago. She is dressed in a one-piece cloth wrapped around her. She too, looks like a wild one, and she is carrying a broom and a duster with which she immediately begins to dust and sweep. Then suddenly she stops and just stands dreamily. Meanwhile,* BOY *enters from upper right and quietly steals behind her and cries 'Hei!' She is startled.*]

GIRL: [*Turning round to face* BOY] How you frightened me.
BOY: Have you just started working in here? And why were you standing there like that?
GIRL: That is none of your business.
BOY: I don't know what is happening in this house. I am sure there are more people here than in Oguaa town. Yet nothing gets done.
GIRL: But you!
BOY: I what? Is this the hour you were instructed to come and clean the place up?
GIRL: Well, that is not my fault.
BOY: What is not your fault? Look at those arms. I wonder what they could do even if you were not so lazy. Listen, today is Friday and Father is going to come in here. And don't stand there staring at me.

GIRL: And anyway, are you the new overseer? Why don't you leave me alone?

BOY: [*Playfully pulling her nose*] I won't!

GIRL: You! [*She raises her arm to hit him, and causes one of the decorative plates to fall. It breaks.* BOY *is furious.*]

BOY: God, what is wrong with you? Look at what you've done!

GIRL: Well, it's broken, isn't it? I wouldn't fuss so much if I were you.

BOY: Doesn't anything bother you?

GIRL: Not much. Certainly not this plate.

[*She bends down to pick up the pieces. Then she stands up again.*]

This mistress will not miss it. After all, she has no time these days for things like plates.

BOY: You are mad, that's all. I thought she said we should always call her 'Mother' and the master 'Father'.

GIRL: [*Giggling*] Some Mother and Father, heh!

BOY: I don't think I have said anything for you to laugh at.

GIRL: You are being very unfair. You know I like both of them very much. [*Earnestly*] I wish I really was their child . . . born to them. [*She pouts.*] As for her too.

BOY: What has happened now?

GIRL: Nothing. Now she flits about like a ghost, talking to herself. [*They stop and listen. The* BOY *moves up to upper left and peeps*] Is she coming?

BOY: [*Not turning round*] No. [*Then he moves back towards* GIRL]

GIRL: Listen, they were saying at the fish-kilns that she went and stared at Takoa's baby so hard that the baby is having convulsions . . .

BOY: [*Shocked*] Ow!

GIRL: Takoa is certainly telling everyone that Mistress, I mean Mother, is swallowing the baby because she is a witch.

BOY: Hei! [*The* GIRL *is startled. The* BOY *moves closer to face her and begins hitting her lips with the fourth finger of his right hand*] Don't let me catch you repeating any of the things those awful women say about Mother.

GIRL: Yes, grandfather.

BOY: And you, where did you hear all these things from?

GIRL: [*Petulantly*] I said at the kilns [*throwing her mouth at him*]. Or are you deaf?

BOY: I am not deaf but people in this house talk too much.

GIRL: It is because of this new affair. And the truth is, she herself talks more about it than anyone else. Whenever she thinks she is alone anywhere, she begins 'O my husband, what have I done, what have I done?' [*She imitates someone puzzled and asks the questions with her hands. Then she giggles.*]

BOY: Don't laugh. Have you seen how you yourself will end? [*He picks her duster up and begins to dust around.*]

GIRL: *Ei*, don't turn wise on me. [*Noticing him working*] Good. You should dust since you're keeping me from doing my work . . .

BOY: Huh! . . . And are you not a woman too?

GIRL: [*Promptly and loudly*] And if I am? [*She lets fall the broom, and looks up for some time without saying anything.*]

BOY: I did not say you can now rest.

GIRL: [*Quietly and to herself*] If I had more money than I knew what to do with, but not a single child, I should be unhappy. If my man refused to talk to me, I should soon start talking to myself; if he would not come to my room or allow me in his, I should pace around in the night. [*She now turns to look at the* BOY.] And after killing myself for him, he said to me one day, go away, and would not tell me why, I should then die of surprise!

BOY: People do not die of surprise.

GIRL: See if I do not.

BOY: [*Whispering*] What do you think is going to happen now?

GIRL: Do I know? All I know is that if she goes away, I shall run away too.

BOY: I shall come with you.

GIRL: [*Coyly*] Not if you would be scolding me all the time . . .

BOY: [*Drawing near her and trying to touch her breasts*] No, I shall not.

[*The* GIRL *hits his hand away. They stand still for a moment. Then they resume working with vigour. The* BOY *begins to whistle some tune.*]

GIRL: And the way she carries on with everyone here . . .

BOY: Playing with us as though we were her kinsmen?

GIRL: Yes; perhaps that is why the master wants to send her away.

BOY: Maybe; and she certainly is more poorly dressed than some of us.

GIRL: Yes, that is another thing. Can't she do something about herself?

BOY: What, for instance?

GIRL: Ho, does she not see her friends, how they go around? All those new and fashionable nkabasroto and bubas? The sleeves blowing out in the wind, the full pointed shoes and the stockings . . .

BOY: Of course, that is what *you* would like . . .

GIRL: Why, if I were her, what would I not do,
what would I not have?
As much as my eye will fancy
and the best my heart desires?

[*She forgets she should be working and lets fall the broom. Her eyes light up with joyful expectation and she acts out her dream to the amazed fascination of* BOY.]

Nkente to sit in for all my work days.
Velvets for visiting. Silks for Sundays.

[ANOWA *enters unnoticed and stands at the door. She looks as she did in the last scene, but wizened now and shabby. She is wearing her old cloth and is barefooted. Her hair is cropped close.*]

GIRL: O if I were her, and she were me
Jewels on my hair, my finger and my knee
In my ears the dangles, on my wrists the bangles
My sandals will be jewelled, my hair will be dressed;
My perfumes will be milled, my talcums of the best.
On my soups I will be keen
No fish-heads to be seen
O for her to be me
So that I could be free!

[ANOWA *glides out unseen. The* BOY *and the* GIRL *stand looking at each other. The* GIRL's *eyes glisten with unshed tears while the* BOY *breathes deeply and loudly a couple of times.*]

BOY: Being a woman, of course, that's all you would think about. Though if I were you and so beautiful, I would not worry. Perhaps Father will take you for wife.
GIRL: *Chiaa, aa,* that man who is afraid of women?
BOY: Listen, it is dangerous talking to you. How can you say a fearful thing like that?
GIRL: But I am not lying . . . they say . . . they say . . .
BOY: Shut up. [*He hits her on her buttocks, runs down lower right and away with the* GIRL *pursuing him, her broom raised. From upper left,* ANOWA *re-enters the hall.*]
ANOWA: [*To the now disappeared* GIRL *and* BOY] You said it right, my child. But the elders gave the ruling before you and even I came: 'The string of orphan beads might look better on the wrist of the leopard but it is the antelope who has lost his mother.'

[*She wanders round aimlessly humming to herself. Presently, Panyin-na-Kakra enter. They are about eight years old. They run in from upper right with ostrich feather fans, stand on either side of the gilded chair and automatically begin fanning the chair. This goes on for some time without* ANOWA *noticing it. When she does, she laughs out dryly.*]

ANOWA: Poor children, I feel like picking them up and carrying them on my back.
PANYIN-NA-KAKRA: [*Still fanning*] Mother please, we did not hear you.
ANOWA: It is all right, my children, I was not speaking to you. [*Aside*] They are fanning that chair now so that by the time their lord enters, the space around it will be cool. I suppose this is one of the nice things Yaako is teaching them to do. Hmm . . . woe the childless woman, they warn. Let someone go and see their mother, who is she? Where is she sitting while they stand here fanning an empty chair? Let someone go and see how she suffered

111

bearing them. The nine months dizziness, when food
tasted like dung and water like urine. Nine months of
unwholesome desires and evil dreams. Then the hour of
the breaking of the amnion, when the space between her
life and her death wore thin like a needy woman's hair
thread. O the stench of old blood gone hot . . . Did she go
through all that and with her rest at the end postponed
so they [*pointing at the boys*] will come and fan an empty
chair? To fan an empty chair? [*She gets up and listlessly goes
to the picture of Queen Victoria and addresses it.*]
Hei, sister, I hear you are a queen. Maybe in spite of the
strange look of you, you are a human woman, too, eh?
How is it with you over there? Do you sometimes feel like
I feel, that you should not have been born? Nana . . .
won't you answer? If you won't answer [*making gesture of
riddance*] take your headache . . . and I say, you don't
have to look at me like that because I have seen your likes
before. [*To herself*] But I shall not cry. I shall not let him
see the tears from my eyes. Someone should have taught
me how to grow up to be a woman. I hear in other lands a
woman is nothing. And they let her know this from the
day of her birth. But here, O my spirit mother, they let a
girl grow up as she pleases until she is married. And then
she is like any woman anywhere: in order for her man to
be a man, she must not think, she must not talk. O—o,
why didn't someone teach me how to grow up to be a
woman? [*Then she remembers the children.*] *Hei*, Kakra,
Panyin! Stop fanning that chair.

PANYIN-NA-KAKRA: [*Startled*] But please, Mother, Yaako
said . . .

ANOWA: I say. Stop fanning that chair Panyin, go and tell
Yaako that I have asked you to stop fanning the chair.
[*They put their fans on one of the stools and* PANYIN *goes out.*
ANOWA *puts her arms around* KAKRA *and moves down with
him. When she sits down he sits on a rug by her.*] Kakra.

KAKRA: Mother.

ANOWA: Where do you and Panyin come from?

KAKRA: The house in Tantri, Mother.

ANOWA: No, I mean before that.

KAKRA: Mother, I don't know.

ANOWA: Kakra, am I growing old?

KAKRA: [*He turns to look at her and then looks away bewildered.*] Mother, I don't know.

ANOWA: No, you don't know. Go and play with your friends, child.

[KAKRA *rises up and leaves.* ANOWA *bows down her head.* KOFI AKO *enters on the arm of* BOY. *He is bedecked as in the last scene.* ANOWA *stares contemptuously at the two of them.* BOY *leads him to the chair and places him in it. Now and any other time in the rest of the scene, when* KOFI AKO *silently examines his limbs, 'Asem yi se nea mokobo tuo' or any African funeral march or drums should be played.*]

BOY: Father, shall I go and fetch Nana the priest?

KOFI AKO: [*Hurriedly*] Not yet. I shall call you and send you with a message for him.

BOY: Yes, Father. [*He retires.*]

[*Awkward silence.*]

ANOWA: I was told that you wanted to speak to me.

KOFI AKO: All I want to say Anowa, is that I do not like seeing you walking around the house like this.

ANOWA: You don't like seeing me walk around the house like what?

KOFI AKO: Please, stop asking me annoying questions.

ANOWA: Don't shout. After all, it is you who are anxious that the slaves should not hear us. What I don't understand, Kofi, is why you want to have so many things your own way.

KOFI AKO: [*Very angrily*] And I don't think there is a single woman in the land who speaks to her husband the way you to do me [*Sighs and relaxes*] Why are you like this, Anowa? Why? [ANOWA *laughs*] Can't you be like other normal women? Other normal people? [ANOWA *continues laughing, then stops abruptly.*]

ANOWA: I still don't know what you mean by normal. Is it abnormal to want to continue working?

KOFI AKO: Yes, if there is no need to.

ANOWA: But my husband, is there a time when there is no need for a human being to work? After all, our elders said that one never stops wearing hats on a head which still stands on its shoulders.

KOFI AKO: I do not see the reason why I should go walking through forests, climbing mountains and crossing rivers to buy skins when I have bought slaves to do just that for me.

ANOWA: And so we come back to where we have been for a long time now. My husband, we did not have to put the strength of our bodies into others. We should not have bought the slaves . . .

KOFI AKO: But we needed them to do the work for us.

[ANOWA *begins to pace up and down and from side to side and never stops for too long any time during the rest of the scene.*]

ANOWA: As though other people are horses! And now look at us. We do nothing from the crowing of the cock to the setting of the sun. I wander around like a ghost and you sit, washed and oiled like a . . . bride on show or a god being celebrated. Is this what we left Yebi for? Ah, my husband, where did our young lives go?

KOFI AKO: [*Angrily*] Stop it, Anowa, stop it. And what is the meaning of all this strange talk? If you feel old, that is your own affair. I feel perfectly young.

ANOWA: Do you?

KOFI AKO: [*Fiercely*] Yes, I do. And you stop creeping around the house the way you do. Like some beggar. Making yourself a laughing stock. Can't you do anything to yourself? After all, you are my wife.

ANOWA: Am I your wife? What is there to prove it?

KOFI AKO: I don't understand you.

ANOWA: Don't you? I am asking you what I do or what there is about me that shows I am your wife. I do not think putting on fine clothes is enough.

KOFI AKO: Are you referring to the fact that we have not had children?

114

ANOWA: An adopted child is always an adopted child and a
    slave child, a slave . . . Perhaps I am the barren one. But
    you deserve a son; so Kofi, I shall get you a wife. One of
    these plump mulatto women of Oguaa . . .
KOFI AKO: Anowa, Stop that!
ANOWA: Besides, such women are more civilised than I, who
    only come from Yebi. They, like you, have learned the
    ways of the white people. And a woman like that may be
    attractive enough to be allowed into your bed . . .
KOFI AKO: Anowa stop that! Stop it, stop it!
ANOWA: [*Laughing*] Stop what? Stop what?

[KOFI AKO *sighs again and relaxes. He begins to examine his
limbs as the funeral music or drums rise and fall, and* ANOWA
*plays at digging her toes into the skins or re-arranging the plates
on the sideboard.*]

And what did the priest say the last time he was here?
KOFI AKO: What do you mean? What has that to do with you?
ANOWA: Too much. I know all this has something to do with
    what he has been telling you.
KOFI AKO: You are speaking as if your head is not there.
ANOWA: [*Screaming*] What did his divination say about me?
KOFI AKO: I don't know. And anyway, listen. I thought you
    were just as good at this sort of thing as he is. You should
    know, should you not? Why don't you go and wash your
    mouth so you can be a priestess at last. I can't stand any
    more of your strange ways.
ANOWA: [*Voice betraying nervousness*] What are you talking
    about?
KOFI AKO: [*Laughing bitterly*] What am I talking about!

[*Another awkward pause*]

ANOWA: Yes, what are you talking about?
KOFI AKO: [*With an almost feigned fatigue*] Please, just leave me
    alone. O God, Anowa did you have to destroy me too?
    What does someone like you want from life? Anowa, did
    you . . . I mean did you make me just to destroy me?

115

ANOWA: Kofi, what are you saying?

KOFI AKO: Anowa, Anowa, O, Anowa.

ANOWA: So what did the priest say the last time he was here?

KOFI AKO: That has nothing to do with you.

ANOWA: I think it has. Too much, I feel deep inside me that all this business about me leaving you has something to do with what he told you last week.

KOFI AKO: What mad talk!

ANOWA: [*Hysterically*] What did the priest's divination say about me?

KOFI AKO: Please stop walking up and down. It irritates me.

ANOWA: Why are you sending me away from you?

KOFI AKO: Just leave me alone.

ANOWA: What have I done wrong?

KOFI AKO: Nothing.

OSMA: Is it because I did not give you children?

[*Silence. She moves up to him and changes her attitude to one of supplication.*]

Do you want to take a new wife who would not like to see me around?

KOFI AKO: Anowa, why do you want to go on asking foolish questions to which you know I cannot give you answers?

ANOWA: But they are not foolish questions.

KOFI AKO: [*Unconcerned*] In fact, I thought you would be glad to get away. I don't know what you want, and even if I knew, I am not sure it would have been in my power to give it. And you can't give me the only thing I want from you, a child. Let us part, Anowa.

ANOWA: But going away is one thing. Being sent away is another.

KOFI AKO: And by that you mean, as always, that you have a right to do what you like and as always I am to sit by and watch?

ANOWA: [*She throws up her hands in despair.*] O the god of our fathers! Is there nothing I can open my mouth to say which cannot be twisted around my own neck to choke me?

116

[*Music or drums as* KOFI AKO *examines his limbs.* ANOWA *paces up and down. Then she speaks, almost to herself.*]

ANOWA: Did the priest say . . . what is there about me which he thinks will not bring you blessings now? I must have done something wrong. I must have done something. I'm not a child. Kofi, I know they say a man whose wife is constantly sleeping with other men does not prosper. Did the priest say I am doing something like that? Or anything as evil as that?

KOFI AKO: [*A bitter smile on his lips*] Just go away and leave me alone, woman.

ANOWA: [*Sadly*] I cannot, my husband. Because I have nowhere to go. I swore I would not go back to Yebi. And I can still live here, can I not? I would not disturb you. I can stay in my part of the house. Just don't send me away, we have not seen each other's beds for far too long for it to matter if we don't any more . . .

[*She stares at him and utters her next words as though she has just made a discovery.*]

ANOWA: A—h—h or is it a death you are dying? We are dying. Listen, my husband, did the priest say you are dying, I am dying, we are dying?

KOFI AKO: You are mad. I am very alive.

ANOWA: [*She gets up and raises her voice*] Boy!

KOFI AKO: Why are you calling him?

ANOWA: It has nothing to do with you.

BOY: [*Running in*] Mother, I am here.

ANOWA: Boy, I am going to ask you a question. [*She resumes pacing up and down.*] Boy, you know your master says I must go away from here and never come back. [BOY *hangs his head down with embarrassment.*] My feet are on the road already and if it were not that he has not yet told me what he has found wrong with me or what I have done wrong, I would already be gone. Boy, do you know why?

BOY: No, Mother.

117

ANOWA: Boy, have you heard of a man who seeks to divorce his wife and will not say why?

BOY: Mother, I have never known the customs of this land well.

ANOWA: What about where you came from? Did you hear of such a case before you were taken away?

BOY: I do not remember that I did.

ANOWA: Boy, I thank you. Go call for me as many of the older men and women as are around . . . Bring everybody on whom your eyes fall.

BOY: Yes, Mother. [*He leaves.*]

KOFI AKO: [*Furiously*] Anowa, what are you doing? Why must they know about this? You have never behaved like a child before—why are you behaving like one now?

ANOWA: I do not know why we must not bring them in. I need their help and they also came from places where men live, eat and die. Perhaps one is among them who can help me. And I am behaving like a child now because I have gained nothing from behaving like a grown-up all my life.

KOFI AKO: [*Surprised*] You are mad Anowa.

ANOWA: Not yet!

BOY: [*From doorway*] Are they to come?

ANOWA: Let them come.

[BOY *re-enters followed by as many men and women as possible. The last pair is the twins. They all shuffle around looking wide-eyed.*]

ALL: Mother, we are here.

ANOWA: I see you. Listen. Has any of you heard of a woman whose husband wanted to divorce her but would not tell her why? [*They look bewildered and answer 'No' as if it were a line in a musical round, sung softly: No, no, no, no, no, no . . . They all whisper aloud to each other.*] Then please you may go . . . [*They all turn round at once.*] No wait . . . Eh—eh . . . I would like to send some of you. I am sending you to the oldest and wisest people on this land; go ask them if they have ever heard of a man who sought to divorce his wife and would not tell her why. [*Points at random to different people*] You go to the bearded woman of Kwaakrom and you to the old priests of Nanaam Mpow. You over there to Bekoe, he whom dwarfs abducted and taught the mysteries of the woods. Go quickly and come back today and walk as you have never walked before. Come quickly, for already I hear too many noises in my head and you must come back before my mind flies and gets lost. [*The crowd disperses through all available exits. Exhausted but still excited,* ANOWA *paces around* KOFI AKO *who is now very silent.*] I have known this was coming for weeks and I have feared. An old man said, 'Fear "it-is-coming" but not "It-has-come" '. But for me 'It-has-come' has brought me no peace. Perhaps . . . Boy!

BOY: [*Running*] Mother, I am here.

ANOWA: I hear Nana Abakframpahene Kokroko is here. He and the other chiefs are meeting with the Governor. Go. Whisper in his ears that he is to come to me. Tell him it is urgent and he is to pardon us for not going to him ourselves. All shall be explained in time. He is to come but without his retinue.

KOFI AKO: [*Raising himself up*] Anowa, what are you doing all this for?

ANOWA: The times are past when our individual actions had to be explained to each other.

[BOY *looks away in embarrassment.*]

KOFI AKO: Perhaps you are going out of your senses.

ANOWA: That should not mean anything to you.

KOFI AKO: That is not what concerns me, but you shall not let this out before Nana. [*He stamps his feet.*]

ANOWA: Just sit there and look at me.

KOFI AKO: [*Shouts*] You may go away, Boy. Forget what your Mother told you.

BOY: Yes Father. [*He retires.*]

ANOWA: Who are you to say what you shall allow and what you shall not allow me?

KOFI AKO: [*Loud with anger*] Nana is my friend and not yours.

119

ANOWA: That is why I am asking him to come.

KOFI AKO: Anowa, you shall not disgrace me before him.

ANOWA: Darkness has overtaken us already, and does it matter if we hit each against the other? Are you not disgracing me before the whole world?

KOFI AKO: Your strange speeches will not persuade me . . .

ANOWA: I am not trying to. It is a long time since my most ordinary words ceased to have any meaning for me.

KOFI AKO: I say once more that Nana is the only man in this world I respect and honour.

ANOWA: My good husband, in the old days how well I knew you. That is why I want to consult him too.

KOFI AKO: I should have known that you were always that clever.

ANOWA: And certain things have shown that cleverness is not a bad thing.

KOFI AKO: Everyone said you were a witch. I should have believed them.

ANOWA: [*Derisively*] Why, have I choked you with the bone of an infant?

KOFI AKO: Stop all this show and just leave me alone, I say.

ANOWA: Then I shall ask advice of whom I please.

KOFI AKO: Anowa, if you do not leave me quietly, but go consulting anybody about this affair, I shall brand you a witch.

ANOWA: [*Shocked*] No!

KOFI AKO: [*Brought suddenly to life by her exclamation*] And if I do, you know there is more than one person in the world who would believe me.

ANOWA: [*Screams*] No, no, no!

KOFI AKO: And there will be those who would be prepared to furnish proof.

ANOWA: Kofi, I am not hearing you right.

KOFI AKO: And then you know what could happen. But, that should not make much difference to you. Since you do not care to live or behave like everybody else . . .

ANOWA: But what have I done?

KOFI AKO: I just want you to leave me, that's all.

ANOWA: O the Gods of my fathers, what is it? What is it?

KOFI AKO: I shall have the little house built for you, as I promised, but in Yebi . . .

ANOWA: But I cannot go and live there.

KOFI AKO: I will give you half of the trade and half of the slaves, if you want them.

ANOWA: I don't want anything from you.

KOFI AKO: Take away with you all the jewelry.

ANOWA: I say I want nothing . . .

KOFI AKO: And you must leave immediately. I myself shall come to Yebi, or send people you can respect to come and explain everything to your family . . .

ANOWA: No, no, no!

KOFI AKO: . . . I shall ask a few men and women to go with you now, and carry your personal belongings.

ANOWA: But . . .

KOFI AKO: Boy!

ANOWA: Stop!

KOFI AKO: What? [*Unknown to the two, not only* BOY *but several of the slaves, men and women, appear.*]

ANOWA: You cannot send me away like this. Not to Yebi, or anywhere. Not before you have told me why. I swore to Mother I was not returning. Not ever. [*Not shedding a tear but her eyes shining dangerously*] No, I am not in rags. But . . . but I do not have children from this marriage. Ah! Yes, Kofi, [*she moves to him and whispers hoarsely and audibly*] we do not have children, Kofi, we have not got children! And for years now, I have not seen your bed. And Kofi, [*getting hysterical*] now that I think back on it, you have never been interested in any other woman . . .

KOFI AKO: What are you saying, Anowa?

ANOWA: Kofi, are you dead? [*Pause*] Kofi, is your manhood gone? I mean, you are like a woman. [*Pause*] Kofi, there is not hope any more, is there? [*Pause*] Kofi . . . tell me, is that why I must leave you? That you have exhausted your masculinity acquiring slaves and wealth?

[*Silence*]

Why didn't you want me to know? You could have told

121

me. Because we were friends. Like brother and sister.
You just did not want me to know? And the priest said it
was my fault. That I ate your manhood up? Why did he
say I did it? Out of envy? Did he not tell you that perhaps
you had consumed it up yourself acquiring wealth and
slaves?

[KOFI *looks around and sees the peeping eyes. He is horrified. He
gestures to* ANOWA *who doesn't know what is happening and
goes on talking. He makes an attempt to go away and then sits
down again. The slaves disappear.*]

ANOWA: Now I know. So that is it. My husband is a woman
now. [*She giggles.*] He is a corpse. He is dead wood. But
less than dead wood because at least, that sometimes
grows mushrooms . . . Why didn't you want me to know?
[*Long pause while they look at each other strangely. Then he gets
up to leave.*] Where are you going? Kofi, don't leave.
[*Pause*] Let us start from the beginning. [*Long pause*] No, I
shall leave you in peace. [*Pause*] I am leaving, Kofi. I am
leaving. I shall leave you in peace.

[*He exits upper left. She watches his receding back until he
disappears. She then shifts her gaze to the gilded chair. She stares
at that for some time, after which her eyes just wander in general
around the room. Then at some point she begins to address the
furniture.*]

ANOWA: Ah, very soon the messengers will be coming back,
Rugs, pictures, you, chair and you, Queen,
Should they ask of me from you, tell them I am gone,
Tell them it matters not what the wise ones say,
For
Now, I am wiser than they.

[*She fixes her eyes on the gilded chair again. Suddenly she jumps
a step or two and sits in it and begins to dangle her legs like a
child, with a delighted grin on her face. She breaks into a giggle.
There is a sudden gun-shot off stage, followed by a stillness. As*

*pandemonium breaks out off stage with women and men
shrieking,* ANOWA *beings to giggle again. The light dies slowly
on her.*

    *Lights come on both parts of the stage. Upper is still the great
hall. In the centre is the gilded chair unoccupied. In the
background can be heard funeral drums and wailing. A few
women, led by* BADUA, *who is weeping, troop in from upper right
and sit down,* BADUA *in the right hand corner nearest the lower
stage. The women sit around the gilded chair as though it is the
funeral bed. A little later,* OSAM *enters from upper left to sit in
the left hand corner facing* BADUA. *All are in deep red
mourning. The drum and wailing stops, but only to give way to
Kofi's* HORNBLOWER *who enters immediately after* OSAM, *stands
directly behind the chair, blows a sequence of the exhortation and
stops. The lights go dim on the upper stage.*
THE-MOUTH-THAT-EATS-SALT-AND-PEPPER *enters.* OLD
WOMAN *first and almost shrieking.*]

OLD WOMAN: *Puei, puei, puei!* This is the type of happening out
    of which we get stories and legends. Yebi, I wish you *dué,
    dué dué.* May all the powers that be condole with you. Kofi
    Ako shoots himself and Anowa drowns herself! This is
    too much. Other villages produce great men, men of
    wealth, men of name. Why should this befall us? What
    tabooed food have we eaten? What unholy ground have
    we trodden?

[OLD MAN *enters, stands in the centre of the stage with his head
down.*]

O Kofi Ako! Some say he lost his manhood because he
was not born with much to begin with; that he had been a
sickly infant and there always was only a hollow in him
where a man's strength should be. Others say he had
consumed it acquiring wealth, or exchanged it for
prosperity. But I say that all should be laid at Anowa's
doorstep. What man prospers, married to a woman like
Anowa? Eh, would even Amanfi the giant have retained
his strength faced with that witch? They say she always

worked as though she could eat a thousand cows. Let the gods forgive me for speaking ill of the dead, but Anowa ate Kofi Ako up!

OLD MAN: [*Looking at her keenly, he chuckles.*] There is surely one thing we know how to do very well. And that is assigning blame when things go wrong.

OLD WOMAN: What do you mean by that! I did not shoot Kofi Ako, did I?

OLD MAN: I never said you did.

OLD WOMAN: Was it not that Anowa who made him shoot himself?

OLD MAN: [*Quietly and not looking at* OLD WOMAN] Perhaps, perhaps, perhaps. And yet no one goes mad in emptiness, unless he has the disease already in his head from the womb. No. It is men who make men mad. Who knows if Anowa would have been a better woman, a better person if we had not been what we are?

[OLD WOMAN *glares at him, spits and wobbles out coughing harder than ever before.*]

They used to say here that Anowa behaved as though she were a heroine in a story. Some of us wish she had been happier and that her life had not had so much of the familiar human scent in it. She is true to herself. She refused to come back here to Yebi, to our gossiping and our judgements. Osam and Badua have gone with the others to bring the two bodies home to Yebi. Ow, if there is life after death, Anowa's spirit will certainly have something to say about that!

[*He begins to walk away, while all the lights begin to die.*]

In the approaching darkness, we hear the single Atentenben wailing in loneliness.